# JOANNA FARROW'S
## Q U I C K   &   E A S Y
# C A K E
## D E C O R A T I N G

*About the author*

J oanna Farrow trained as a home economist before
spending several years working on various
women's magazines. With two small children, Joanna
now works freelance. She has written several cookery
books, including *Quick & Easy Fish Cookery*.

*BBC BOOKS'
QUICK & EASY
COOKERY SERIES*

Launched in 1989 by Ken Hom and Sarah Brown,
the *Quick & Easy Cookery* series is a culinary win-
ner. Everything about the titles is aimed at quick
and easy recipes – the ingredients, the cooking
methods and the menu section at the back of the
books. Eight pages of colour photographs are also
included to provide a flash of inspiration for the
frantic or faint-hearted.

# JOANNA FARROW'S
## QUICK & EASY
# CAKE
## DECORATING

BBC BOOKS

Published by BBC Books,
a division of BBC Enterprises Limited,
Woodlands, 80 Wood Lane
London W12 0TT

First published 1994
© Joanna Farrow 1994
The moral right of the author has been asserted
ISBN 0 563 36905 1
BBC Quick & Easy is a trademark of
the British Broadcasting Corporation.

Designed by Peter Bridgewater
Photographs by Philip Webb
Home Economist: Joanna Farrow
Illustrations by Lorraine Harrison

Set in Bembo by Create Publishing Services Ltd, Bath

Printed and bound in Great Britain by Clays Ltd, St Ives plc
Colour separation by Technik Ltd, Berkhamsted
Colour sections printed by Lawrence Allen Ltd,
Weston-super-Mare
Cover printed by Clays Ltd, St Ives plc

# CONTENTS

# INTRODUCTION

F or anyone who feels the desire to create something completely original, cake decorating at any level is one of the more realistic ways of doing so. At one end of the scale is the simply iced sponge decorated with flowers and ribbons, and at the other the most elaborate work of art, lovingly and laboriously crafted; both give the creator a tremendous sense of achievement. This book deals with the 'simply iced' cakes, those that are interesting enough to spark attention at any occasion, yet quick enough for the most frantically busy enthusiast.

The book is divided into chapters on Useful Equipment, Store-cupboard, Basic Cakes and Icings, followed by the cake designs themselves. The Equipment chapter lists all you'll need, however basic, to create the finished cake. Similarly, the Store-cupboard chapter gives a run-down of the ingredients that might crop up in the book. Both the equipment and the ingredients have been selected with convenience in mind. The object of the book would be defeated if you had to spend days tracking down an illusive flower cutter or icing paste. The basic cakes, whether sponge, fruit or chocolate are included for anyone who really wants a home-made cake. If this is the case, it's best baked a day or more in advance, as fruit cakes take several hours to cool and sponges are easier to cut if they've sat overnight. Although I've suggested which basic cakes to use in the cake design chapters, they're almost entirely interchangeable. Just remember that firmer cakes withstand shaping better than a soft sponge.

If time is a problem you might prefer to buy a cake to decorate, particularly if it's for a child's birthday. The difficulty with using bought cakes is that they tend to be very small. This can be solved by securing several slabs of cake together with jam or buttercream, and cutting them down to size if necessary.

The Icings chapter also gives basic recipes which take very little time to make. Here again, you can save time by buying moulding icing. I would thoroughly recommend this when you only need small quantities. You might, however, prefer making it yourself for larger cakes (see p. 30).

The fun starts with the design chapters. These are divided into cakes for children, adults, special occasions and those made with chocolate. Some are simplicity itself, while others take a little longer. Generally the decorating (once cake and icing are prepared) will take between about 30 minutes and a couple of hours. Bear in mind, however, that we all work at different speeds, and in most busy kitchens there are frequent interruptions. One great advantage cake decorating has over other forms of food preparation is that it can be left while you attend to another more urgent cause, and then returned to when time allows.

For the sake of presentation, there are a few finishing touches that I always like to add. Covering the cake board with a thin layer of icing adds colour and sometimes enhances the theme. Likewise, tying a ribbon around the board completes the effect. Neither of these is essential and can be omitted if you're looking for further shortcuts.

I hope that this book illustrates how anyone with the will can master cake decoration and may even be inspired to attempt something at a more advanced level. I can say from my own experience that the more involved you get in cake decorating the more you'll want to experiment and develop this rewarding hobby.

## NOTES ON THE RECIPES

All eggs used in the recipes are size 3 unless otherwise stated. Follow one set of measurements only. Do not mix imperial and metric. All measuring spoon quantities are level. Ovens should be pre-heated to the temperature specified.

# STORE-CUPBOARD

Most of us go and buy the ingredients we need to make and ice a cake when the occasion arises, but there are plenty of sugars, pastes, ready made icings, etc. with a long storage life, which can be kept ready at hand for whenever you want them. The following is a list of ingredients that you need for icing and decorating cakes, rather than in the baking itself. Most are widely available alongside baking goods in supermarkets. You might, however, have to look further afield, in kitchenware stores and cake decorating shops, for good quality food colourings. Don't be put off if you haven't a supplier near you, most provide a convenient mail order service (see p. 108).

### APRICOT JAM

Sieved and warmed apricot jam is brushed over fruit and sponge cakes to act as a 'glue' for the marzipan or icing. Marmalade or honey works equally well.

### BOUGHT DECORATIONS

Both supermarkets and cake decorating shops stock a wide selection of ready-made decorations. These range from small icing flowers, figures and seasonal motifs bought in cake decorating shops to the more everyday adornments stocked at the supermarkets. These include vermicelli, dragées, sugar strands, crystallized fruits and candy sweets, which appeal in particular to children.

### COCOA POWDER

A dusting of cocoa powder over a white chocolate or pale cream cake makes an effective finishing touch.

### CHOCOLATE

Chocolate can be divided into four main groups, all of which come in plain, milk and white varieties.

Couverture, the finest and most expensive, has the best flavour and a rich, glossy sheen. Before use it has to be heated and cooled to precise temperatures so it is generally left to the specialists.

Cooking chocolate is stocked in the supermarkets, but the quality varies considerably depending on how much cocoa butter it contains, i.e. the more the better. It is ideal for melting and using in cakes.

Dessert chocolate, the type sold in confectioners' has a good flavour but is fractionally more expensive and remains quite thick when melted.

Chocolate-flavoured cake covering should not be confused with cooking chocolate. It contains very little cocoa butter and has a fatty taste and texture. Despite this it melts well and makes excellent chocolate curl decorations (see Chocolate caraque on p. 47).

### COFFEE

A useful stand-by when you're stuck for a flavouring for cream or buttercream. Blend the powder or granules with the smallest quantity of hot water to make the coffee dissolve before use.

### CORNFLOUR

Ordinary cornflour, most commonly used to thicken sauces and gravies, gives moulding icing a beautifully smooth finish when dusted over the surface with the palms of the hands. If you've bought the icing but forgotten the cornflour, icing sugar makes an adequate substitute.

### DRIED EGG WHITE

A great stand-by when you want to ice a cake but discover you've run out of eggs. This pasteurized dried egg albumen comes in powder form and is quickly reconstituted with water to take the place of fresh egg whites for royal and moulding icing. It keeps for several months and takes up very little space.

### FOOD COLOURINGS

Food colourings are now available in every colour imaginable. While cake-making enthusiasts tend to build up a huge collection of exciting colours, you can achieve numerous colour variations by blending the most basic colours together. Food colours can be divided into three basic types.

Liquid colours are sold at the supermarket in a range of primary colours. These are water based, not very concentrated and difficult to knead into moulding icing. They only produce strong shades when added to glacé icing, royal icing and buttercream.

Good quality paste and concentrated liquid colours come in small pots from department stores and cake specialists. Add to icing a little at a time using a cocktail stick and be particularly cautious if you want a very subtle colour.

Powder colours are used to create soft shading and tinting on elaborate cakes. They're usually brushed onto the hardened icing using a fine paint-brush, particularly on moulded or piped flowers.

### FOOD FLAVOURINGS

Supermarkets stock a wide selection of flavourings like rum, almond, orange, peppermint, etc. for adding to cakes and icings. These should be used cautiously as they have a synthetic flavour and, in most cases, it's just as easy to add the real thing. Natural vanilla essence or extract, used sparingly, is pleasant in sponges, cream and butter icings. Better still buy vanilla-flavoured sugar, or keep a vanilla pod in a jar of caster or icing sugar for several weeks until the vanilla pod gives the sugar a lovely flavour and aroma. Substitute some of this sugar for ordinary sugar in cakes and icings.

### ICING PENS

These look just like felt-tip pens, but are filled with edible food colour and come in a wide choice of colours. Use to write names or make patterns directly onto hardened icing but plan your design first as mistakes cannot be erased.

### ICING SUGAR

Usually available in 450 g (1 lb) or 900 g (2 lb) quantities. Unless the sugar has been stored in moist conditions it usually flows from the bag as a fine powder which won't need sifting.

### LIQUID GLUCOSE

Along with egg whites and icing sugar, liquid glucose makes up the highly versatile Moulding icing (see p. 30). Unfortunately there's no substitute, so if you intend to make lots of cakes, buy plenty – it stores well.

### MARZIPAN/ALMOND PASTE

A layer of marzipan or almond paste is traditionally used to cover a rich fruit cake before adding the icing, but it makes an equally effective decoration for those who find icing too sweet. Unless you particularly want the deep yellow-coloured paste, choose the white which can then be coloured as you would icing. Like moulding icing it can also be shaped into novelty decorations.

**NUTS**

Whole, chopped or powdered, nuts frequently come up in cake and icing recipes. Mixed whole nuts, glazed with jam or caramel make a mouthwatering topping. Keep an eye on 'use by' dates as they do become stale.

**PIPING JELLY**

This has a half-set jelly consistency and, because of its translucency, is great for adding a 'wet look' effect to water on novelty cakes. (See the Penguin party cake on p. 50.) It's only available from cake decorating shops but an imitation can be made by gradually blending 1 teaspoon arrowroot with 6 tablespoons water and heating until thickened.

**READY-TO-PIPE ICINGS**

Sold under the name of 'decorating' or 'writing' icing these are perfect for quick 'fun' cakes. The icing comes in a tube with a fine point for writing or line designs, or with a choice of interchangeable nozzles. You won't achieve a highly professional-looking finish but the results are instant and effective.

**READY-TO-ROLL ICING**

There are several brands of this ready-made icing which is simply rolled like pastry and smoothed over a cake or moulded like plasticine into smaller decorations. Although it has a more distinctive flavour than home-made Moulding icing (see p. 30) it's equally versatile and can be used as a speedy alternative in any of the recipes in this book. Before use you may need to work in a little extra icing sugar as some brands are quite soft, sticky and difficult to work with in a warm kitchen. Cake decorating shops sell ready-to-roll icing in large quantities, sometimes already coloured, which may work out cheaper if you're decorating several large cakes. Always store tightly wrapped in several layers of cling film or foil as the icing quickly develops a hard crust if left exposed. Unopened or tightly wrapped ready-to-roll icing will keep for several months. Use the 'Best before' date as a guide.

**ROYAL ICING**

Sold in 450 g (1 lb) packs, bought royal icing combines icing sugar with dried egg white, and it simply needs beating with a little water before using. It can be spread smoothly, swirled or piped onto cakes. Unopened or properly sealed royal icing sachets will keep for several months in a cool, dry place.

# USEFUL EQUIPMENT

One of the most inviting aspects of quick and easy cake decorating is that you needn't spend a fortune on specialist equipment. Most of the cakes in this book can be successfully made using the gadgets and tools already stocked in the average kitchen. Listed below are some items that come up again and again in the recipes, so that if you haven't got them already, you might consider buying them. And if this whets your appetite, it might encourage you to visit a cake decorating shop which will be an Aladdin's cave of gadgets, tools, decorations, icings and all sorts of intriguing items. If you don't have a shop near you, try mail order – see the specialist suppliers on p. 108.

## CAKE BOARDS

Thin cake cards, or thicker cake boards come in a huge variety of shapes and sizes. Neither is absolutely essential for many of the cakes in this book, but they do provide a perfectly flat base which can be covered attractively with icing. You may prefer to use one when transporting the cake to a party or other special occasion.

## COCKTAIL STICKS

These are really useful for adding fine decorative lines to icing and getting into corners that spoons and fingers can't reach. They're also good for dotting food colours onto icing. (Use a clean stick each time you change colour to avoid making a mess of your food colouring pots.)

## CUTTERS

A variety of metal and plastic cutters, from tiny *petit four* sizes to large biscuit ones, are widely available. Cake decorating shops also stock a wide range of miniature cutters from simple blossom to those for specific flowers. The most easy to use are those which come with an ejector spring. Once the flower has been cut out the spring is pushed, effortlessly releasing the delicate flower cut-out. This dispenses with the problem of small icing shapes sticking stubbornly to the cutters, and consequently speeds up the whole process. Small cutters can be used to impress designs into soft icing – see Quick & Easy Decorative Ideas on p. 45 – while larger ones can be used to make cut-out decorations for securing to cakes.

### DECORATIVE SCRAPERS

Usually made from plastic, these come with a variety of decorative edges, usually zig-zag. When gently scraped around the sides of the cake they leave a textured design.

### EMPTY BOXES

Not necessary for the making of the cake but worthwhile having ready if the cake is to be transported. Secure the base of plate or cake board to the box with plasticine or Blu-tack to prevent the cake from slipping around. On a wet day, cover the box loosely with greaseproof as drops of rain will dissolve the icing.

### ICING SMOOTHER

For cakes covered with moulding icing the palms of the hands are used to 'smooth out' the icing. Bought plastic 'icing smoothers' are generally used by serious cake decorators to complete the task, giving the icing a perfectly flat finish and smooth sheen. Very effective and easy to use, they're a worthwhile investment if you're decorating a cake with a large flat surface, e.g. the Bows and garlands cake on p. 97. Once you've covered the cake with moulding icing brush the smoother with cornflour and use a dusting action over the top of the cake. Finish by smoothing around the sides.

### KITCHEN PAPERS/CLING FILM/FOIL

Cling film is ideal for tightly wrapping moulding icing while not in use, and to cover the surface of royal or glacé icing to prevent a crust forming. Foil is used to wrap cakes and keep them fresh if made in advance. Crumpled up, it provides a surface on which moulded flowers and other decorations can be left to harden into realistic shapes. Greaseproof paper is used to make piping bags and line tins.

*To line a tin with greaseproof,* place the required tin on the greaseproof paper and draw around the base with a pencil. Cut out just inside the marked line. For sides of the tin cut a long strip, the circumference of the tin and slightly deeper than the sides. Make a 1 cm (½ in) fold down one long side then make snips along this edge up to the fold line (see drawing 1). Brush the tin with melted butter or margarine then press the strip of paper around the sides so that the snipped edge sits on the base. Press the cut out square or circle of paper into base and then brush all the sides again (see drawing 2).

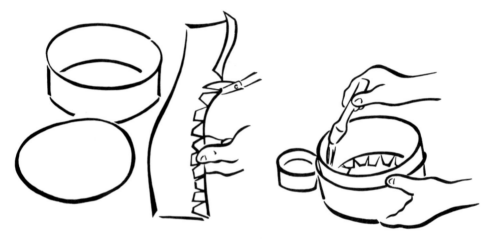

1 *Make snips up to the fold line along the edge of the greaseproof paper.*

2 *Brush the greaseproof paper with melted butter.*

*To line the base of a pudding basin or mixing bowl,* cut out a circle of paper slightly larger than base of bowl. Make 1 cm (½ in) cuts from the edges of the circle towards the centre. Grease bowl and press paper circle into base.

### MEASURING SPOONS

A set of ordinary kitchen measuring spoons is worth having when accurate measurements are needed e.g. for baking powder, spices, or water.

### PAINTBRUSHES

A fine paintbrush is useful for simple decorative details and for dampening small pieces of icing before securing to the cake.

## PALETTE KNIFE

A good 'bendy' palette knife makes light work of spreading icing, cream, buttercream or chocolate over a cake.

## PIPING BAGS

Cloth or nylon piping bags are useful for piping large quantities of buttercream or whipped cream, but for small decorative details, a greaseproof bag (see below) is cheaper, less wasteful and easier to handle. If you tend to make lots of cakes, put your feet up in front of the television and make plenty of these bags in one go.

*To make a paper piping bag*, cut out a 25 cm (10 in) square from greaseproof or waxed paper. Fold this in half diagonally to make a triangle. Holding the centre of the long folded edge with one hand bend the right-hand point of the triangle round to meet the centre point (see drawing 1). Bring the left-hand point over in the opposite direction so that all the points meet, forming a cone (see drawing 2). Fold the points over several times to secure the cone. Cut a very tiny tip off the end of the bag if using to pipe lines. Alternatively cut off a 5 mm (¼ in) tip and fit with a piping nozzle.

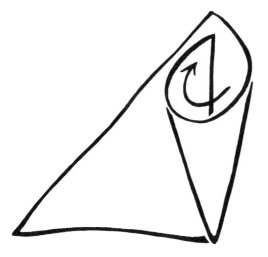 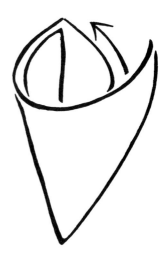

*1 Bend the right-hand point round to meet the centre point.*

*2 Bring the left-hand point over in the opposite direction so that the three points meet.*

## PIPING NOZZLES

There are dozens of metal piping nozzles available for cake decorating. These range from the most delicate 'writer' nozzles which barely have a hole visible at the end to those used for stars, basketwork and petal shapes. The most you'll need in the following chapters is a medium star and writer nozzle, although writing and plain lines can be worked from a greaseproof bag from which you've snipped off the very tip (see above).

## RIBBONS

A length of ribbon to fit the depth of the cake board can give a professional-looking finishing touch to a special occasion cake. Secure to board at the back of the cake using dressmakers' pins.

## ROLLING-PIN

Cake decorating shops sell nylon rolling-pins with a perfectly smooth finish for rolling out moulding icing. An ordinary pastry pin in good condition can be substituted. For small quantities of icing, a child's toy rolling-pin is ideal.

## SHARP KNIFE

A small fine-bladed knife is best for cutting cleanly through moulding icing when making decorations.

## TURNTABLE

Not essential for *Quick & Easy* cakes but a worthwhile investment if you intend to make plenty. The cake can be revolved easily as you go from one detail to another, and large cakes become much more manoeuvrable. A large, upturned bowl makes a handy substitute as long as you check that it remains well balanced.

# BASIC CAKES

B irthdays, parties and other special occasions have a way of creeping up on the cook, who suddenly realizes that there's a lot to be done, and no time to do it. I find that having the basic cake made, even if it is just a simple sponge, gives me the satisfaction that I am at least partially organized and all set to start icing it at the next opportunity. On the following pages are several recipes for the easiest cakes you could wish for, including rich and light fruit cakes, a moist chocolate cake, Madeira and quick cake mix. All of them can be made to any size, following the quantities chart beside the appropriate recipe. In most cases they can be used as the basis of any of the decorated cakes in the following chapters. (You might need to adapt the decoration slightly if you've made a 25 cm/10 in cake instead of the 20 cm/8 in cake suggested in the recipe.) I've also included a 'servings' guide as a rough indication of how many the cakes will serve, although this will depend largely on general appetites, whether everyone's eating the cake after a huge feast, and who's given the task of cutting it!

# RICH FRUIT CAKE

Although usually reserved for Christmas and weddings, there's no reason why rich fruit cakes shouldn't be made for a birthday or special gift. This is an 'all-in-one mix' version of a traditional, and usually time-consuming, rich fruit cake recipe and the results are just as good. The most important tip is to avoid overcooking, so test the cake about 15 minutes before the end of the suggested cooking time. Gently press the surface, it should feel firm, and a skewer inserted into the centre should come out cleanly. If uncooked cake is visible on the skewer, return to the oven for a little longer. Unlike sponge cakes, rich fruit cakes need long, slow cooking, so if you make the cake in the evening and realize that you'll be up half the night waiting for it to cook, don't worry. Simply cover the tin with cling film and store in a cool place overnight ready for cooking on the following day. Once baked, leave the cake to cool in the tin then drizzle the surface with brandy. Wrap in a double thickness of foil if you're not going to decorate the cake immediately. Tightly wrapped and stored in a cool, dry place, a rich fruit cake will keep well, maturing in flavour, for up to a year. Once decorated it can be kept for a further month, although the icing will gradually become brittle and difficult to cut.

**INGREDIENTS**

*For ingredients, cake tin sizes, cooking times and servings see chart opposite.*

Pre-heat the oven to gas mark 1, 275°F (140°C). Grease and line base and sides of chosen tin with greased, greaseproof paper (see p. 14).

Place the butter or margarine, sugar, flour, mixed spice and eggs in a large bowl and beat well with a wooden spoon or electric whisk until creamy. Add the mixed dried fruit, cherries and nuts and stir well until combined.

Turn the mixture into the prepared tin and level the surface. Bake in the centre of the oven for time stated. Leave to cool in tin.

| | | | | | | |
|---|---|---|---|---|---|---|
| ROUND TIN | 15 cm (6 in) | 18 cm (7 in) | 20 cm (8 in) | 23 cm (9 in) | 25 cm (10 in) | 28 cm (11 in) |
| SQUARE TIN | 13 cm (5 in) | 15 cm (6 in) | 18 cm (7 in) | 20 cm (8 in) | 23 cm (9 in) | 25 cm (10 in) |
| BUTTER OR MARGARINE, SOFTENED | 100 g (4 oz) | 150 g (5 oz) | 185 g (6½ oz) | 250 g (9 oz) | 375 g (13 oz) | 425 g (15 oz) |
| DARK MUSCOVADO SUGAR | 100 g (4 oz) | 150 g (5 oz) | 185 g (6½ oz) | 250 g (9 oz) | 375 g (13 oz) | 425 g (15 oz) |
| PLAIN FLOUR | 150 g (5 oz) | 175 g (6 oz) | 225 g (8 oz) | 350 g (12 oz) | 450 g (1 lb) | 550 g (1¼ lb) |
| GROUND MIXED SPICE | 1 teaspoon | 1 teaspoon | 1½ teaspoons | 2 teaspoons | 1 tablespoon | 4 teaspoons |
| EGGS | 2 | 3 | 3 | 4 | 6 | 8 |
| MIXED DRIED FRUIT | 400 g (14 oz) | 550 g (1¼ lb) | 750 g (1¾ lb) | 1 kg (2¼ lb) | 1.5 kg (3 lb) | 1.7 kg (3¼ lb) |
| CHOPPED GLACÉ CHERRIES | 50 g (2 oz) | 50 g (2 oz) | 75 g (3 oz) | 90 g (3½ oz) | 150 g (5 oz) | 175 g (6 oz) |
| CHOPPED MIXED NUTS | 25 g (1 oz) | 25 g (1 oz) | 40 g (1½ oz) | 50 g (2 oz) | 75 g (3 oz) | 100 g (4 oz) |
| BAKING TIME | 1½–2 hours | 2–2¼ hours | 3–3¼ hours | 3½–3¾ hours | 4 hours | 4½–4¾ hours |
| SERVINGS | 14 | 18 | 24 | 30 | 40 | 50–60 |

**19**

# LIGHT FRUIT CAKE

If you like fruit cake but find the rich fruit version just too much, this semi-rich variation might be the answer as it can be decorated just as you would a richer cake. It keeps well for up to a month and, for a special occasion, can be drizzled with brandy after baking. If you prefer a nutty flavour, omit the cherries and substitute the same quantity of chopped walnuts, almonds or brazil nuts. To test whether the cake is cooked remove it from the oven 15 minutes before the end of the suggested cooking time. If cooked, the surface should feel firm, and a skewer, inserted into centre, should come out cleanly. If uncooked cake is visible on the skewer, return to the oven for a little longer.

**INGREDIENTS**

*For ingredients, cake tin sizes, cooking times and servings see chart opposite.*

Pre-heat the oven to gas mark 1, 275°F (140°C). Grease and line the base and sides of chosen tin with greased, greaseproof paper (see p. 14).

Place the butter or margarine, sugar, flour, mixed spice and eggs in a large bowl and beat well with a wooden spoon or electric whisk until creamy. Add the mixed dried fruit and cherries and stir well until combined.

Turn the mixture into the prepared tin and smooth the surface, making a depression in the centre of the mixture. Bake in the centre of the oven for time stated. Leave to cool in tin.

| ROUND TIN | 15 cm (6 in) | 18 cm (7 in) | 20 cm (8 in) | 23 cm (9 in) | 25 cm (10 in) | 28 cm (11 in) |
|---|---|---|---|---|---|---|
| SQUARE TIN | 13 cm (5 in) | 15 cm (6 in) | 18 cm (7 in) | 20 cm (8 in) | 23 cm (9 in) | 25 cm (10 in) |
| BUTTER OR MARGARINE, SOFTENED | 175 g (6 oz) | 225 g (8 oz) | 275 g (10 oz) | 400 g (14 oz) | 450 g (1 lb) | 550 g (1¼ lb) |
| LIGHT MUSCOVADO SUGAR | 175 g (6 oz) | 225 g (8 oz) | 275 g (10 oz) | 400 g (14 oz) | 450 g (1 lb) | 550 g (1¼ lb) |
| PLAIN FLOUR | 225 g (8 oz) | 275 g (10 oz) | 350 g (12 oz) | 450 g (1 lb) | 550 g (1¼ lb) | 750 g (1½ lb) |
| GROUND MIXED SPICE | 1 teaspoon | 1½ teaspoons | 2 teaspoons | 1 tablespoon | 4 teaspoons | 2 tablespoons |
| EGGS | 3 | 4 | 4 | 5 | 6 | 7 |
| MIXED DRIED FRUIT | 275 g (10 oz) | 400 g (14 oz) | 450 g (1 lb) | 750 g (1½ lb) | 900 g (2 lb) | 1.2 kg (2½ lb) |
| CHOPPED GLACÉ CHERRIES | 50 g (2 oz) | 50 g (2 oz) | 75 g (3 oz) | 100 g (4 oz) | 150 g (5 oz) | 175 g (6 oz) |
| BAKING TIME | 1½–1¾ hours | 1½–2 hours | 2¼–3 hours | 3¼–3½ hours | 3½–3¾ hours | 4 hours |
| SERVINGS | 12 | 16 | 20 | 25 | 30 | 35–40 |

# QUICK CAKE MIX

With this versatile recipe you can bake a cake that's similar in taste and texture to the classic Victoria sandwich, but prepared in half the time. It's light, moist and very easy to make, and with a choice of simple flavourings, is perfect for a child's birthday cake. Follow the ingredient quantities closely as too little baking powder will not produce sufficient rise, while too much will make the cake sink in the middle. As with any sponges, cook the cake as soon as it's mixed as the raising agent starts to react as soon as it comes into contact with moisture. To test if the cake is cooked, gently press the surface – it should feel firm. Once made, decorate within a day or two as sponges do not have the keeping qualities of a fruit cake. Alternatively make in advance and freeze for up to a month.

**INGREDIENTS**

*For ingredients, cake tin sizes, cooking times and servings see chart opposite.*

Pre-heat the oven to gas mark 3, 325°F (160°C). Grease and line the base of chosen tin with greased, greaseproof paper (see p. 14).

Place all the ingredients in a large bowl and beat with a wooden spoon or electric whisk until creamy. Stir in flavouring if using. Turn the mixture into the prepared tin and level the surface. Bake in the centre of the oven for time stated on p. 23. Leave to cool slightly in tin then transfer to a wire rack to cool completely.

| | | | | | | |
|---|---|---|---|---|---|---|
| ROUND TIN | 15 cm (6 in) | 18 cm (7 in) | 20 cm (8 in) | 23 cm (9 in) | 25 cm (10 in) | 28 cm (11 in) |
| SQUARE TIN | 13 cm (5 in) | 15 cm (6 in) | 18 cm (7 in) | 20 cm (8 in) | 23 cm (9 in) | 25 cm (10 in) |
| BUTTER OR MARGARINE, SOFTENED | 100 g (4 oz) | 175 g (6 oz) | 225 g (8 oz) | 275 g (10 oz) | 350 g (12 oz) | 450 g (1 lb) |
| CASTER SUGAR | 100 g (4 oz) | 175 g (6 oz) | 225 g (8 oz) | 275 g (10 oz) | 350 g (12 oz) | 450 g (1 lb) |
| EGGS | 2 | 3 | 4 | 5 | 6 | 8 |
| SELF-RAISING FLOUR | 100 g (4 oz) | 175 g (6 oz) | 225 g (8 oz) | 275 g (10 oz) | 400 g (14 oz) | 550 g (1 ¼ lb) |
| BAKING POWDER | ½ teaspoon | 1 teaspoon | 1 teaspoon | 1 ½ teaspoons | 2 teaspoons | 1 tablespoon |
| BAKING TIME | 40 minutes | 50 minutes | 1 hour | 1 ¼ hours | 1 ¼ hours | 1 ½ hours |
| SERVINGS | 6–8 | 10 | 14 | 18 | 20 | 24 |
| FLAVOURINGS | | | | | | |
| LEMON, ORANGE OR LIME RIND, GRATED | ½ fruit | 1 fruit | 2 fruits | 3 fruits | 3 fruits | 4 fruits |
| COCOA POWDER (SUBSTITUTE FOR SAME QUANTITY OF FLOUR) | 15 g (½ oz) | 20 g (¾ oz) | 25 g (1 oz) | 25 g (1 oz) | 40 g (1 ½ oz) | 50 g (2 oz) |
| SULTANAS | 25 g (1 oz) | 40 g (1 ½ oz) | 50 g (2 oz) | 65 g (2 ½ oz) | 75 g (3 oz) | 100 g (4 oz) |

# MADEIRA CAKE

A traditional Madeira cake is a firm, but moist, buttery tea-time cake that has a lovely lemony flavour and strips of lemon peel decorating the surface. I've included it in this book because its firm texture lends itself perfectly to cutting and shaping into novelty cakes like the Bag of sweets on p. 52. At the same time, it makes a good base for covering with marzipan and icing for those who don't like fruit cakes. Make a plain Madeira cake or choose from the flavourings at the bottom of the ingredients chart below. Once made, Madeira cake will keep in a cool dry place for up to a week. Covered with marzipan or icing it will store well for a further two weeks.

**INGREDIENTS**

*For ingredients, cake tin sizes, cooking times and servings see chart opposite.*

Pre-heat the oven to gas mark 3, 325°F (160°C). Grease and line the base and sides of chosen tin with greased, greaseproof paper (see p. 14).

Place all the ingredients in a large bowl and beat well with a wooden spoon or electric whisk until creamy. Stir in flavouring if using. Turn the mixture into the prepared tin and level the surface. Bake in the centre of the oven for time stated or until the surface feels firm and a fine skewer inserted into the centre comes out cleanly. Leave to cool slightly in tin then transfer to a wire rack to cool completely.

| ROUND TIN | 15 cm (6 in) | 18 cm (7 in) | 20 cm (8 in) | 23 cm (9 in) | 25 cm (10 in) | 28 cm (11 in) |
|---|---|---|---|---|---|---|
| SQUARE TIN | 13 cm (5 in) | 15 cm (6 in) | 18 cm (7 in) | 20 cm (8 in) | 23 cm (9 in) | 25 cm (10 in) |
| BUTTER OR MARGARINE, SOFTENED | 100 g (4 oz) | 175 g (6 oz) | 275 g (10 oz) | 400 g (14 oz) | 450 g (1 lb) | 550 g (1¼ lb) |
| CASTER SUGAR | 100 g (4 oz) | 175 g (6 oz) | 275 g (10 oz) | 400 g (14 oz) | 450 g (1 lb) | 550 g (1¼ lb) |
| EGGS | 2 | 3 | 5 | 7 | 8 | 10 |
| SELF-RAISING FLOUR | 175 g (6 oz) | 225 g (8 oz) | 350 g (12 oz) | 450 g (1 lb) | 550 g (1¼ lb) | 750 g (1½ lb) |
| LEMON JUICE | 1 tablespoon | 2 tablespoons | 3 tablespoons | 4 tablespoons | 5 tablespoons | 6 tablespoons |
| BAKING TIME | 1–1¼ hours | 1¼–1½ hours | 1½–1¾ hours | 1¾–2 hours | 2 hours | 2–2¼ hours |
| SERVINGS | 8 | 12 | 16 | 20 | 24 | 30 |
| FLAVOURINGS | | | | | | |
| CHOPPED AND TOASTED MIXED NUTS | 25 g (1 oz) | 50 g (2 oz) | 75 g (3 oz) | 100 g (4 oz) | 150 g (5 oz) | 175 g (6 oz) |
| GLACÉ CHERRIES | 50 g (2 oz) | 65 g (2½ oz) | 75 g (3 oz) | 90 g (3½ oz) | 100 g (4 oz) | 150 g (5 oz) |

# MOIST CHOCOLATE CAKE

O f all the chocolate cake recipes I've come across, this recipe is the most delicious. It's very chocolatey, moist and because melted chocolate is added, it won't dry out during cooking as do many chocolate cakes made solely with cocoa powder. If the cake is for a special occasion, drizzle it with brandy, rum or orange-flavoured liqueur before covering with icing. Store for up to a week un-iced, and for a further week once decorated.

**INGREDIENTS**

*For ingredients, cake tin sizes, cooking times and servings see chart opposite.*

Pre-heat the oven to gas mark 3, 325°F (160°C). Grease and line the base and sides of chosen tin with greased, greaseproof paper (see p. 14).

Place the milk and lemon juice in a jug and leave to stand while preparing the cake mixture. Break up the chocolate into a bowl. Stand the bowl over a saucepan of gently simmering water and leave until melted. Place the butter or margarine, sugar, eggs, flour, bicarbonate of soda and cocoa in a large bowl. Add half the milk and lemon mixture (this will have separated slightly). Beat the mixture well using a wooden spoon or electric whisk. Add the melted chocolate and the remaining milk and beat again until the ingredients are combined.

Turn the mixture into the prepared tin. Bake in the centre of the oven for time stated or until the cake is well risen and a fine skewer, inserted into the centre, comes out cleanly. Leave to cool in tin.

| ROUND TIN | 15 cm (6 in) | 18 cm (7 in) | 20 cm (8 in) | 23 cm (9 in) | 25 cm (10 in) | 28 cm (11 in) |
|---|---|---|---|---|---|---|
| SQUARE TIN | 13 cm (5 in) | 15 cm (6 in) | 18 cm (7 in) | 20 cm (8 in) | 23 cm (9 in) | 25 cm (10 in) |
| MILK | 120 ml (4 fl oz) | 175 ml (6 fl oz) | 250 ml (8 fl oz) | 325 ml (11 fl oz) | 450 ml (15 fl oz) | 600 ml (1 pint) |
| LEMON JUICE | 1 teaspoon | 2 teaspoons | 1 tablespoon | 4 teaspoons | 2 tablespoons | 3 tablespoons |
| PLAIN CHOCOLATE | 50 g (2 oz) | 75 g (3 oz) | 100 g (4 oz) | 175 g (6 oz) | 225 g (8 oz) | 350 g (12 oz) |
| BUTTER OR MARGARINE, SOFTENED | 50 g (2 oz) | 75 g (3 oz) | 100 g (4 oz) | 175 g (6 oz) | 225 g (8 oz) | 350 g (12 oz) |
| CASTER SUGAR | 100 g (4 oz) | 175 g (6 oz) | 225 g (8 oz) | 350 g (12 oz) | 450 g (1 lb) | 750 g (1½ lb) |
| EGGS | 1 | 1 | 2 | 3 | 4 | 6 |
| SELF-RAISING FLOUR | 150 g (5 oz) | 200 g (7 oz) | 275 g (10 oz) | 450 g (1 lb) | 650 g (1 lb 6 oz) | 900 g (2 lb) |
| BICARBONATE OF SODA | ½ teaspoon | ¾ teaspoon | 1 teaspoon | 1½ teaspoons | 2 teaspoons | 3 teaspoons |
| COCOA POWDER | 1 tablespoon | 4 teaspoons | 2 tablespoons | 3 tablespoons | 4 tablespoons | 6 tablespoons |
| BAKING TIME | 1 hour | 1¼ hours | 1½ hours | 1¾–2 hours | 2¼ hours | 2½–2¾ hours |
| SERVINGS | 8 | 12 | 16 | 20 | 24 | 30 |

# ICINGS

This is where the fun starts – the cake's baked, the decoration has been chosen and you're eager to tackle the icing! There are literally dozens of different icings, glazes, pastes and creams frequently used in cake decorating. From these, I've selected a few of the most popular, versatile and easy to use.

Top of the list is Moulding icing (see p. 30). If you haven't used it before, now's the time to take advantage of its marvellous qualities. Both bought or home-made versions work well on any of the cakes in this book. You might find it useful to experiment with a packet of bought icing (the ready-to-roll variety) to get an idea of how the paste should feel to work with, before making your own.

Royal icing (see p. 29) is also popular, particularly on fruit cakes. While a professional cake decorator would not dream of coating a cake with icing without a protective layer of marzipan in between, it's perfectly acceptable for a quick and easy cake. This said, you can easily add a layer of marzipan first if you have the time and inclination.

Both moulding and royal icing are the perfect choice for any organized cook. Fruit cakes covered with either will store in a cool, dry place for several weeks, while sponge cakes will keep, uncut, for up to two weeks.

For covering chocolate cakes there's a delicious Chocolate ganache (see p. 41). This is a chocolate cream that's used both in *pâtisserie*-style desserts and cakes, but adapts equally well to cake decorating. Bear in mind that when you cover a cake with an icing that contains cream it won't store for more than a few days in the refrigerator, or overnight in a very cool place. Buttercream-covered cakes keep surprisingly well (again, in a very cool place) but don't have the shelf-life of a cake covered with moulding or royal icing.

# ROYAL ICING

For most of us, royal icing turns up once a year in the form of 'peaked snow' on the Christmas cake. It does, however, have other uses in cake decorating, both for simple piped work and as an alternative cake covering for rich fruit or light fruit cakes. To detract from the sweetness, I've used far more lemon juice than would normally be added. This improves the flavour but makes the icing set hard more quickly – not a problem with most cakes as they're devoured before the icing has had a chance to set. If, however, the cake is to be stored the lemon juice can easily be reduced.

Any left-over royal icing can be stored, tightly wrapped, in the refrigerator. Thinned down with fruit juice or water, it can also be spread over a sponge or small cakes. For the quantities chart covering all sizes see below.

### INGREDIENTS

*1 egg white*
*2 teaspoons lemon juice, strained*
*225 g (8 oz) icing sugar*

Place the egg white and lemon juice in a large bowl and beat with a wooden spoon or electric whisk until frothy. Gradually beat in the icing sugar, beating well after each addition until the icing holds its shape and forms soft peaks. (You may not need to add all the icing sugar.)

Cover the surface of the icing with cling film to prevent a crust forming, until ready to use.

| | | | | | | |
|---|---|---|---|---|---|---|
| ROUND CAKE | 15 cm (6 in) | 18 cm (7 in) | 20 cm (8 in) | 23 cm (9 in) | 25 cm (10 in) | 28 cm (11 in) |
| SQUARE CAKE | 13 cm (5 in) | 15 cm (6 in) | 18 cm (7 in) | 20 cm (8 in) | 23 cm (9 in) | 25 cm (10 in) |
| EGG WHITE | 2 | 2 | 4 | 4 | 6 | 6 |
| LEMON JUICE | 2 teaspoons | 2 teaspoons | 1 tablespoon | 1 tablespoon | 4 teaspoons | 4 teaspoons |
| ICING SUGAR (QUANTITY REFERRED TO IN INGREDIENTS FOR CAKE DESIGNS) | 450 g (1 lb) | 450 g (1 lb) | 900 g (2 lb) | 900 g (2 lb) | 1.5 kg (3 lb) | 1.5 kg (3 lb) |

# MOULDING ICING

Whether you call it modelling paste, sugar paste, fondant or any other name, this rollable, mouldable icing is one of the most versatile, fun aspects of cake decorating. It's particularly suited to quick and easy cakes, replacing the laborious 'flat' icing of a smart cake, yet offering more versatility than everyday buttercream or glacé icing. For a simple celebration cake, nothing could be simpler than covering a cake with moulding icing, tying a wide ribbon around the sides and finishing the top with a spray of fresh flowers. This simple idea could be colour co-ordinated to complement the colours of the flowers. Moulding icing itself is easily coloured by dotting with food colouring, preferably paste, and kneading in. Interesting effects can be made by only partially kneading in colour so that, when rolled out, the icing has a marbled look, see the Ancient ruin cake on p. 84. Alternatively colour separate pieces of moulding icing with different colours, break into small pieces and lump together. Once rolled the icing will be mottled with colour.

Even more fun can be had with shaping moulding icing. It can be modelled into virtually anything. Let your creative talents take over!

This recipe is a home-made version of bought ready-to-roll icing and is used in exactly the same way. The advantages of making your own is that it's slightly cheaper if made in large quantities and it tastes a little better. Either can be used for the decorations in this book, but do remember to keep any unused moulding icing tightly wrapped in cling film as it quickly dries out if left exposed. Left-overs will keep for several weeks if wrapped in several thicknesses. Below is a chart showing the quantities of moulding icing you'll need to cover various cake sizes.

**INGREDIENTS**

*1 egg white*
*2 tablespoons liquid glucose*
*450 g (1 lb) icing sugar*
*Cornflour or icing sugar for dusting*

Place the egg white and liquid glucose in a large bowl. Gradually beat in the icing sugar until the mixture becomes too stiff to stir. Turn out onto a surface sprinkled with more icing sugar. Work in the remaining icing sugar until the mixture forms a stiff paste. Wrap tightly until ready to use. If, when rolled, the icing is very sticky and soft, work in some more icing sugar. If dry and cracking, knead in a little water until pliable.

| ROUND CAKE | 15 cm (6 in) | 18 cm (7 in) | 20 cm (8 in) | 23 cm (9 in) | 25 cm (10 in) | 28 cm (11 in) |
| SQUARE CAKE | 13 cm (5 in) | 15 cm (6 in) | 18 cm (7 in) | 20 cm (8 in) | 23 cm (9 in) | 25 cm (10 in) |
| | | | | | | |
| EGG WHITE | 1 | 1 (size 1) | 2 | 2 (size 1) | 3 | 3 (size 1) |
| LIQUID GLUCOSE | 2 tablespoons | 3 tablespoons | 4 tablespoons | 5 tablespoons | 6 tablespoons | 7 tablespoons |
| ICING SUGAR (QUANTITY REFERRED TO IN INGREDIENTS FOR CAKE DESIGNS) | 450 g (1 lb) | 750 g (1½ lb) | 900 g (2 lb) | 1.25 kg (2½ lb) | 1.5 kg (3 lb) | 1.6 kg (3½ lb) |

## TO COVER A CAKE WITH MOULDING ICING

Generously dust the work surface with icing sugar. Roll out the moulding icing, dusting the rolling-pin with icing sugar if the icing sticks, until 10 cm (4 in) larger than the cake. Lift the icing over the cake and smooth over top and sides using hands dusted with cornflour or icing sugar (see drawing 1). Ease the icing around the sides, smoothing with the hands to eliminate any creases. Trim off the excess icing around the base of the cake (see drawing 2).

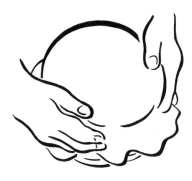

*1 Smooth the icing over the top and sides of the cake with your hands.*

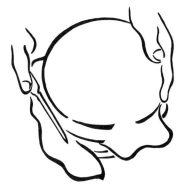

*2 Trim off the excess icing.*

# GLACÉ ICING

G lacé icing has limited uses in cake decorating as it cannot be shaped, moulded or piped, but it does make a good 'glue' for securing decorations, flowers, ribbons, etc. to a cake. It's also made in literally seconds. The easiest mistake when making glacé icing is to add too much water. As a result you end up adding pounds of icing sugar to compensate, and wonder what to do with it all. If using to spread over the top of a cake it's worth substituting lemon or orange juice for the water, the tangy flavour is far more appetizing.

The quantities below are sufficient to cover the top of a 20–23 cm (8–9 in) cake, which is the usual size for this type of icing. Halve the quantities if you're simply using the icing to secure decorations to a special cake.

**INGREDIENTS**

*225 g (8 oz) icing sugar*
*4 teaspoons warm water*

Place the sugar and water in a small bowl. Beat with a wooden spoon until smooth and thick enough to coat the back of the spoon. Beat in a little more water if necessary. Use immediately or cover surface of icing with cling film to prevent a crust forming.

*Front:* BAG OF SWEETS
(*see page 52*)

*Back:* SUNFLOWER
(*see page 64*)

*Front:* SURPRISE PARCEL
(*see page 56*)

*Back:* BIRTHDAY BALLOONS
(*see page 54*)

*Front:* PENGUIN PARTY
*(see page 50)*

*Back:* WINTER WONDERLAND
*(see page 60)*

FLYING KITE
(see page 58)

PIRATE
(*see page 62*)

MONEY MOUNTAIN
*(see page 68)*

PINK TULLE CAKE
(*see page 81*)

ANCIENT RUIN
(*see page 84*)

# CHOCOLATE GANACHE

For chocolate lovers, this must be one of the most irresistible mixtures you could possibly eat – a delicious blend of pure chocolate and cream, flavoured with a splash of liqueur. Freshly made ganache has the consistency of thick cream, ideal for pouring over a cake so that it thickly covers both top and sides in a rich, glossy coat. As ganache cools it thickens, and after whisking it turns paler and creamy enough to be spread or piped over a cake or to use as a filling. Both methods look and taste really good.

The following recipe is enough to coat a 20–23 cm (8–9 in) cake, which is the usual size for this type of icing. If cooled and thickened, you'll have enough icing to split and sandwich the cake too.

**INGREDIENTS**

*175 g (6 oz) plain chocolate*
*175 ml (6 fl oz) double cream*
*1 tablespoon brandy or orange-flavoured liqueur*

Break up the chocolate and place in a bowl with the cream and liqueur. Rest the bowl over a pan of gently simmering water and leave until melted, stirring occasionally until the mixture is smooth.

*To pour over cake*, stand the cake on a rack over a large plate or tray to catch the drips. When the ganache has cooled enough to coat thickly the back of the wooden spoon, pour it over the cake, easing icing around the sides with a palette knife.

*To spread or pipe*, chill the mixture then whisk until it holds its shape. Spread over cake, or pipe using a large piping bag and star nozzle.

# BUTTERCREAM

Although buttercream is most frequently used on everyday cakes, it's surprisingly adaptable to quick, easy 'occasional' cakes, and seems particularly popular with children. It can be flavoured and coloured, piped, spread or textured – and conveniently 'stays put' once you've finished working with it. The only drawback with buttercream is that it does not take some colours easily because of the naturally yellow tinge of the butter. If you want to make a definite colour, substitute white vegetable fat (solid vegetable oil) for the butter or margarine.

To get a light, creamy texture it's best to use really soft butter or margarine, so remove it from the fridge a while before you need it (or pop it in the microwave to soften slightly). The quantity below is enough to sandwich and cover a small sponge cake, but it can easily be increased for larger cakes (see the chart opposite). There's also a list of flavour variations for the basic recipe, so don't forget to increase this too if you're making up a larger batch.

**INGREDIENTS**

*100 g (4 oz) butter or margarine, softened*
*225 g (8 oz) icing sugar*
*2 teaspoons boiling water*

Place the butter or margarine in a bowl and beat lightly with a wooden spoon or electric whisk until softened. Beat in the icing sugar, water and flavouring, if using, until light and fluffy.

| ROUND CAKE | 15 cm (6 in) | 18 cm (7 in) | 20 cm (8 in) | 23 cm (9 in) | 25 cm (10 in) | 28 cm (11 in) |
|---|---|---|---|---|---|---|
| SQUARE CAKE | 13 cm (5 in) | 15 cm (6 in) | 18 cm (7 in) | 20 cm (8 in) | 23 cm (9 in) | 25 cm (10 in) |
| BUTTER OR MARGARINE, SOFTENED | 100 g (4 oz) | 175 g (6 oz) | 175 g (6 oz) | 225 g (8 oz) | 275 g (10 oz) | 350 g (12 oz) |
| ICING SUGAR (QUANTITY REFERRED TO IN INGREDIENTS FOR CAKE DESIGNS) | 225 g (8 oz) | 350 g (12 oz) | 350 g (12 oz) | 450 g (1 lb) | 550 g (1 ¼ lb) | 750 g (1 ½ lb) |
| BOILING WATER | 2 teaspoons | 1 tablespoon | 1 tablespoon | 4 teaspoons | 5 teaspoons | 2 tablespoons |

**FLAVOUR VARIATIONS**

*Vanilla*   Add 1 teaspoon vanilla essence.

*Citrus*   Add the finely grated rind of 1 orange, lemon or lime.

*Chocolate*   Add 15 g (½ oz) cocoa powder.

*Coffee*   Add 1 tablespoon of very strong black coffee or 1 teaspoon coffee essence.

*Liqueur*   Add 2 tablespoons brandy, rum, Amaretto or orange-flavoured liqueur.

*Easy Praline*   Add 50 g (2 oz) ground almonds and 25 g (1 oz) light muscovado sugar.

# CHOCOLATE MODELLING PASTE

When white, milk or plain chocolate is mixed with golden syrup it takes on a texture that's amazingly pliable and great fun to use. This is perfect for moulding neat finishing touches such as simple flowers and ribbons for a special chocolate cake, or, if you're feeling more ambitious, modelling into novelty shapes like teddy bears and small animals. The quantity below is sufficient to make a couple of moulded animals or an elaborate ribbon decoration. For colour contrast you can get even more carried away by combining white and plain chocolate modelling paste.

Although this recipe needs to chill for about an hour before use, it's made in 5 minutes so prepare it before the cake itself and avoid delay at the decorating stage. Any left-overs will keep in the refrigerator for several weeks. Soften at room temperature or pop in the microwave for a few seconds.

**INGREDIENTS**

*100 g (4 oz) plain, milk or white chocolate*
*2 tablespoons golden syrup*

Break up the chocolate into a bowl. Stand the bowl over a saucepan of gently simmering water and leave until melted. Remove from the heat and beat in the golden syrup until the mixture thickens to make a paste. Transfer the paste to a polythene bag and chill for about 1 hour until firm but pliable.

## QUICK & EASY
## DECORATIVE IDEAS

When compiling a book on icing cakes, many decorative ideas spring to mind that don't necessarily warrant the space of a whole recipe. None the less they can make quick, fun, finishing touches that might be very useful on a simple cake. The following ideas are in no particular order and range from small decorative borders to ways in which you might cover an entire cake.

### STIPPLING

Cover a cake with white or pale-coloured Moulding icing (see p. 30). Then dilute some food colouring with water (either a contrasting colour or darker shade of the colour on the cake). Dip a small piece of bathroom sponge in the colour until only just moistened then dab it all over the icing.

### DECORATIVE EMBOSSING

Cover a cake with white or pale-coloured Moulding icing (see p. 30). While the icing is still soft press small biscuit or *petit four* cutters into the icing at regular intervals to leave a shallow impression. These might be hearts, numerals, flowers or figures. Using food colourings and a fine paintbrush, paint the icing inside the shapes.

You can experiment equally well by pressing more unusual shapes into the icing, such as the ends of icing tubes, seashells and even buttons!

### SEARED SUGAR

Colour some icing sugar by cautiously adding a little paste colour and blending in with the back of a teaspoon. Dust over the surface of a cake covered with Moulding icing (see p. 30), Buttercream (see p. 42) or whipped cream. Using oven gloves, hold a metal skewer over the hob until very hot, then gently press the skewer horizontally into the icing. Lift immediately and make more skewer marks, re-heating the skewer as it cools. A diamond pattern is particularly attractive.

### GLAZED FRUIT AND NUTS

This is ideal for those who like the cake but not the icing. Heat several tablespoons of apricot jam in a saucepan then press through a sieve. Use a little to glaze the top of a Madeira or fruit cake (see pp. 24, 18 or 20). Arrange a selection of glacé fruit and nuts, e.g. whole almonds, walnuts, Brazils, cherries, pineapple and stem ginger over the cake, either in lines or decreasing circles. Alternatively scatter the fruits casually. Brush generously with the remaining apricot glaze.

Finish by tying ribbon or a strip of marzipan around the sides of the cake.

### CHOCOLATE LACE

Cover the top and sides of a cake with melted chocolate or Chocolate ganache (see p. 41). Melt a little chocolate in a contrasting colour and place in a paper piping bag (see p. 15). Snip off the merest tip. Holding the bag about 5 cm (2 in) above the cake, pipe random, continuous lines by moving your hand quickly over the cake. Once the top is covered tilt the cake and use the same technique on the sides.

### DIPPED FRUITS

Melt some plain, milk or white chocolate in a bowl over a pan of gently simmering water. Half dip a selection of glacé fruits, one at a time, in the chocolate. Let excess chocolate fall back into the bowl then transfer the coated fruits to a sheet of greaseproof paper until dry.

Use to decorate the top of a cake covered with chocolate, whipped cream or Buttercream (see p. 42). Fresh fruits like strawberries, cherries and grapes also work successfully.

### ICING ROPES

These make an easy but smart decoration on a cake that's been covered with Moulding icing (see p. 30), Royal icing (see p. 29), Buttercream (see p. 42), Chocolate ganache (see p. 41) or marzipan. They can be made from Moulding icing or marzipan. Divide the icing or marzipan in half and knead a different colour into each half. Roll long thin sausage shapes in each colour then twist together to make a rope. Lay around the base or top edge of cake, or alternatively in swags around the sides.

Chocolate modelling paste (see p. 44) also works well using chocolate in contrasting colours.

## FRILLED FLOWERS

Thinly roll out a little plain or coloured Moulding icing (see p. 30). Cut a strip about 2 cm (¾ in) wide and 10 cm (4 in) long. Dust the icing and the end of a cocktail stick with cornflour or icing sugar. Roll the cocktail stick along one edge of the icing strip so that it starts to frill. Once one edge of the strip is completely frilled, dampen the straight edge with water and roll up to create a flower. Make more flowers in the same way, varying the length of the strip to create flowers of different sizes.

## CHOCOLATE CARAQUE

This can be made with proper plain, milk or white chocolate but is easiest with chocolate-flavoured cake covering. Melt about 225 g (8 oz) chocolate and spread over a marble slab or cool, scratch-resistant surface. Leave until set. Using a large sharp knife, draw it across the chocolate at an angle of 45° so that the chocolate rolls into curls. Transfer to a tray while making the remainder.

Use the caraque to decorate the top of a chocolate cake, dusting with icing sugar if preferred.

## CHOCOLATE CUT-OUTS

Melt 100 g (4 oz) plain, milk or white chocolate and spread thinly onto a sheet of greaseproof paper. Tilt the edges of the paper so that the chocolate covers the paper smoothly. Leave the chocolate until hardened but not brittle. Using decorative cutters, cut out shapes from the chocolate, then carefully lift them away from the paper. Use to border a chocolate-covered cake.

Novelty shapes like teddy bears or gingerbread men look effective if you add polka dot 'buttons' in a contrasting colour.

## QUICK BRODERIE ANGLAISE

Cover a cake with Moulding icing (see p. 30) in your chosen colour. While still soft tie a narrow ribbon around the sides about 1 cm (½ in) down from the top edge. Using the point of a knitting needle, make small holes at intervals around the sides of the cake. Fill a paper piping bag (see p. 15) with a little

Royal icing (this should be at 'just peaking' consistency, see p. 29). Snip off the merest tip from the bag and pipe small circles around each hole.

### SUGARED SILHOUETTE

Trace a simple shape, e.g. Christmas tree, star, parcel or flower onto thick paper. Cut out the shape and lay over the centre of a cake covered with Moulding icing (see p. 30), melted chocolate or Chocolate ganache (see p. 41). Sift icing sugar or cocoa powder around the edges of the paper and to the edges of the cake. Carefully lift off the paper to leave the pattern.

### FILIGREE

Cover a cake with white or pastel-coloured Moulding icing (see p. 30). Fill a paper piping bag (see p. 14) with a little Royal icing (see p. 29). (This should be at 'just peaking' consistency.) Snip off the merest tip from the bag. Pipe long, continuous, curvy lines over the top of the cake.

This always looks effective and is good for covering up imperfections in the icing. It can also be done on the icing-covered board around the cake.

### SUGARED BELLS

Mix some caster sugar with a little water until dampened. Pack tightly into a silver bell mould. (The type sold for wedding cake decorations are ideal.) Tap out the sugar, like a sandcastle, onto a sheet of foil. Leave the bells to dry out for 10–20 minutes then carefully scoop out the soft centres with the tip of a teaspoon. (If the bells are too soft to scoop leave for a little longer.) Leave to dry completely.

Arrange in groups of two or three, with ribbon, on a Christmas cake.

# CAKES FOR CHILDREN

Q uick and easy children's cakes are possibly the most fun to make, as children readily appreciate simple designs which bear a resemblance to themes that they are particularly fond of. Whereas adults will notice 'out of proportion' modelling, excessively loud colours and not-quite-perfect icing, children get quite excited by bold designs and bright, almost garish, colours, paying far less attention to the workmanship behind it. In my experience the birthday cake is a crucial part of the party celebrations and children spend days deciding which cake they would most like, and then changing their minds almost hourly. In the end you present them with the one that you'd decided to do in the first place and everyone's happy.

Another appealing aspect of making a child's cake is that younger members of the family can 'help', which ultimately saves you time later in the day. This is a good reason for choosing Moulding icing (see p. 30). To a small child, this icing is rather like plasticine, equally mouldable and messy. The coloured trimmings from the cake can be passed down the work surface so that he or she, with the aid of a small rolling-pin, cutters or blunt knife, can create a small scale masterpiece!

Candles are usually quite important to children on birthday cakes. Although these are used on only a few of the cakes in this chapter they can easily be added to any cake design. If there's no room on the cake itself (or it would spoil the design), simply secure them to the board. First make holes by twisting the tip of a skewer into the board then press the candle holders into the holes. Alternatively roll balls of moulding icing and press the candles into these. Secure to the board with a dampened paintbrush.

On the following pages are some simple cakes designed to suit children of all ages. The Flying kite, Birthday balloons and Penguin party should appeal to most children up to the ages of seven or eight while the Bag of sweets and Surprise parcel might be better for older boys and girls. Perhaps only the Winter wonderland is obviously a 'girlie' cake, while the Pirate might be better suited to a boy. This said, all children are different and have their own individual tastes.

# PENGUIN PARTY

### SERVES

— 16 —

## INGREDIENTS

18 cm (7 in) square
  Madeira cake (see p. 24)
3 tablespoons apricot jam
450 g (1 lb) Moulding
  icing (see p. 30)
Cornflour or icing sugar
  for dusting
225 g (8 oz) Royal icing
  (see p. 29)
Blue food colouring
Icing sugar for dusting
Several small plastic
  penguins
Candles (optional)
2 tablespoons piping jelly
  or 1 quantity arrowroot
  jelly (see p. 11)

It's not only plastic model dinosaurs that have hit most toy shops in a big way. Take a look in the larger stores and you'll see that the shelves are stocked full of animals of every description. This is good news for speedy children's cakes as you can buy several, position them in the appropriate 'icing surroundings', and you have a cake that will not only delight small children but each partygoer can take home a small gift along with a piece of cake. (Have a surplus supply of animals to fill those party bags.) I particularly liked the penguins, and icing icebergs is very easy to copy. (See the photograph on p. 35.) If you prefer, you could easily adapt this idea to 'frogs on a waterlily pond', 'lizards in the desert' or 'dinosaurs in a rocky landscape'. The possibilities are endless!

*Use white icing on the back of a teaspoon to create the foaming waves.*

*1* Cut the cake into about 6 pieces of varying sizes. Make all the cuts very angular so that some pieces have pointed tips. Trim other pieces level so that the penguins can stand on them. Melt the jam in a saucepan, then press through a sieve. Brush over the cakes using the pastry brush.
*2* Roll out the moulding icing on a surface lightly dusted with cornflour or icing sugar. Cover the pieces of cake, one at a time, trimming off any excess icing around the bases. It's best to cover the larger cakes first so that the trimmings can be re-rolled to cover the smaller cakes.
*3* Reserve 1 tablespoon of the royal icing. Colour the remainder blue and spread a very thin layer over the cake board. Position the cakes on the board. Spread the remaining blue icing around the cakes, peaking the icing up around each cake.
*4* Using the back of a teaspoon, touch the blue peaks with the reserved white icing to resemble foaming waves (see drawing).
*5* Decide where the penguins will be positioned. Sprinkle these areas generously with icing sugar then press plenty of penguin foot marks into the icing sugar with the feet of one plastic penguin.
*6* Press the penguins firmly into the cake until securely in place. Press the candles to one side of the pointed cakes.
*7* Using a paintbrush, brush the piping jelly or arrow-root jelly over the sea to give it a 'wet look' effect.

**EQUIPMENT**

*Sharp knife*
*Sieve*
*Pastry brush*
*Rolling-pin*
*30 cm (12 in) hexagonal or square silver cake board*
*Paintbrush*

# BAG OF SWEETS

## SERVES

### — 12 —

**INGREDIENTS**

*18 cm (7 in) round tin
quantity of Moist
chocolate cake (see
p. 26) or Madeira cake
(see p. 24)
Yellow and orange food
colourings
900 g (2 lb) Moulding
icing (see p. 30)
Cornflour or icing sugar
for dusting
225 g (8 oz) Buttercream
(see p. 42)
Large selection of sweets*

The thrill of making this cake is that you can get so absorbed in buying cheap and cheerful sweets in the sort of confectioner's that has a children's selection. All the old favourites like gobstoppers, black jacks, fruit salads, sweet necklaces, lollipops and marshmallow sticks are all worthwhile ingredients, and now there's a much wider choice of equally 'bad for you' sweets. (See the photograph on p. 33.) If it's a while since you've made such a selection (if at all), you might be surprised at the cost, it's not a question of so many chews to the penny any more, as so many chews to the pound. However, a birthday party warrants a cake laden with goodies and this is sure to please a child of any age. It might also suit any adults who haven't quite shed the craving for kids' sweets. I know there are a couple in my family!

The cake itself is baked in an ordinary pudding basin. This is an amazingly successful way of getting a good round shape for novelty cakes. Use either the classic 'Christmas pudding' type of basin or a Pyrex glass bowl.

*Wrap two rectangles of icing around the cake to make the bag.*

*1* Pre-heat the oven to gas mark 3, 325°F (160°C). Grease the pudding basin then line the base with a circle of greaseproof paper (see p. 14). Grease the greaseproof. Turn the cake mixture into the basin and level the surface. Bake for time stated in the cake recipe. Leave to cool in basin, then remove and peel off the paper. Roughly trim off the corners of the cake to give a completely rounded shape.

*2* Using a cocktail stick, dot a little yellow food colouring into 225 g (8 oz) of the moulding icing and knead it in. Roll out on a surface dusted with cornflour or icing sugar. Lightly brush the cake board with water to moisten then lay the icing over the board. Smooth out gently with the palms of the hands then trim off excess around the edges.

*3* Place the cake on the icing and spread with the buttercream using a palette knife.

*4* Colour the remaining icing orange and divide in half. Roll out one half and cut out a 23 × 10 cm (9 × 4 in) rectangle. Brush the edges with water then lift the icing around one half of the cake with dampened edges facing inwards. Roll out the remaining icing and cut out another rectangle the same size. Dampen the edges then lift around the other side of the cake so that the ends meet the first rectangle (see drawing). Pinch the icing together to secure in place.

*5* Fill the cake with sweets, pressing lollies into the cake to secure and letting some sweets hang over the sides. Scatter some sweets around the board.

## EQUIPMENT

*1.5 litre (2 ½ pint) pudding basin*
*Greaseproof paper*
*Cocktail sticks*
*Rolling-pin*
*25 cm (10 in) round silver cake board or drum*
*Sharp knife*
*Palette knife*
*Paintbrush*

# BIRTHDAY BALLOONS

### SERVES

### —— 12 ——

**INGREDIENTS**

*18 cm (7 in) square Quick
cake mix (see p. 22),
Madeira (see p. 24) or
Moist chocolate cake (see
p. 26)
225 g (8 oz) Buttercream
(see p. 42)
225 g (8 oz) Moulding
icing (see p. 30)
Red, blue and green food
colourings
Cornflour or icing sugar
for dusting
Several red 'bootlace'
sweets
Candles and holders*

Covered with buttercream and finished with quickly moulded icing balloons, this is one of the easiest cakes you could make. (See the photograph on p. 34.) To get the long thin shape I halved an 18 cm (7 in) square cake and arranged the pieces side by side, but you can make it any shape or size, depending on the number of birthday guests. Both long, narrow plates and cake boards can be a problem to find. If you get stuck buy a large thin cake card and cut it in half to obtain a long rectangle. This can be covered in shiny coloured paper (the sort that won't show grease marks) to set off the bright colours of the cake.

*Make a pattern of wavy lines in the buttercream
using a cocktail stick.*

*1* Slice the cake in half vertically. Freeze half of one cake for a trifle or dessert (otherwise the finished cake will be too long). Stand the remaining cakes on their sides and secure together with a little buttercream. Place on the rectangular board.
*2* Using a palette knife, cover the top and sides of the cake with the remaining buttercream and spread as smoothly as possible.
*3* Divide the moulding icing into three. Using a separate cocktail stick to dot the colour for each piece, colour a third red, a third blue and a third green. With your hand lightly dusted with cornflour or icing sugar, roll a small ball of red icing, about the size of a large grape, then flatten into a balloon shape with a slightly pointed end. Roll a tiny cone-shaped piece of icing and press a cross into the thick end. Carefully secure the pointed end of the cone to the pointed end of the balloon with a dampened paintbrush.
*4* Gently press the balloon onto the side of the cake. Use the remaining icing to shape more balloons and press into position around the cake. Any left-over icing can be shaped into balloons and positioned around the cake on the plate or board.
*5* Cut lengths of the 'bootlaces' and press into the icing to make the balloon string, not forgetting the balloons lying next to the cake.
*6* Press the candles into the holders and position along the top of the cake.
*7* Using the tip of a cocktail stick mark a pattern of wavy lines into the buttercream (see drawing).

*Rectangular cake plate, card or board, covered if liked*
*Palette knife*
*Cocktail sticks*
*Paintbrush*

# SURPRISE PARCEL

### SERVES
—— 14–24 ——

**INGREDIENTS**

*20 cm (8 in) any square cake (see pp. 18–27)*
*4 tablespoons apricot jam*
*3 contrasting food colourings*
*900 g (2 lb) Moulding icing (see p. 30)*
*Cornflour or icing sugar for dusting*
*1 metre ribbon, at least 5 cm (2 in) wide*
*225 g (8 oz) wrapped chocolates*
*Extra ribbon to decorate (optional)*

When the ribbon is cut on this birthday parcel, a delicious selection of chocolates is revealed inside. (See the photograph on p. 34.) Although included in the children's chapter it really can be made for anyone of any age, by simply 'personalizing' the colour scheme and the chocolates. Virtually any cake base can be used (see Basic cakes chapter) but cut off the 'dome' if excessive, as this would reduce the space that you'll want to fill with chocolates. The number of people that this cake serves will vary according to the richness of the basic cake which you choose. This parcel is decorated with cut out dots, but any other shapes, such as hearts or numerals can be used instead. The only other requirement is very wide ribbon. Floristry or satin ribbon from a haberdashery shop or department store is ideal.

*To make the dots, roll the icing into balls and gently press them into the cavities using your fingertips.*

*1* Cut the cake in half vertically. Melt the jam in a saucepan then press through a sieve. Using a pastry brush, brush over all sides of the cakes except the top surfaces.

*2* Choose a food colouring for covering the cake board. Using a cocktail stick, add it to 225 g (8 oz) of the moulding icing and knead it. (If you prefer, only partially knead in the colour so the icing remains streaky.) Thinly roll out the icing on a surface dusted with cornflour or icing sugar. Lightly brush the cake board with water to moisten, then lay the icing over the board. Smooth down lightly with the palms of the hands then trim off the excess icing.

*3* Reserve 100 g (4 oz) of the moulding icing. Select the food colouring for the parcel and knead into the remaining moulding icing. Cut the icing in half.

*4* Roll out one half and use to cover the glazed sides of one cake half, smoothing icing over the corners and sides using hands dusted with cornflour or icing sugar. Cover the other cake half in the same way.

*5* Using the two cutters, cut out rounds from the icing on the cake. This is easier if you first dip the cutters in icing sugar, push into the icing, then gently pull out with a twisting action. Divide the reserved 100 g (4 oz) of moulding icing in half and colour each differently. Roll into balls and press into the cut out cavities (see drawing).

*6* Lay the strip of ribbon over the board and position the cakes, so that the bases sit on the edges of the ribbon and the un-iced cake sides face inwards.

*7* Fill the centre of the cake with the chocolates then bring the ribbon up over the cake and tie in a bow. You might find it easier to make a separate bow.

*Sieve*
*Pastry brush*
*Cocktail sticks*
*Rolling-pin*
*28 cm (11 in) round silver cake board*
*Sharp knife*
*2.5 cm (1 in) plain cutter or the wide end of a large piping nozzle*
*1 cm (½ in) plain cutter or the wide end of a small piping nozzle*

# *F*LYING KITE

### S E R V E S

—— 14-16 ——

Madeira cake (see p. 24)

or Quick cake mix (see p. 22)

Buttercream (see p. 42)

Moulding icing (see p. 30)

### INGREDIENTS

20 cm (8 in) round
Madeira cake (see p. 24)
or Quick cake mix (see
p. 22)
100 g (4 oz) Buttercream
(see p. 42)
4 tablespoons apricot jam
900 g (2 lb) Moulding
icing (see p. 30)
Blue, brown, green, red
and yellow food
colourings
Cornflour or icing sugar
for dusting
15 cm (6 in) length
liquorice bootlace
Several 'dolly mixtures'
Black food colouring or
dark icing pen

**B**rightly coloured kites seem to enthral most young children, even if they've never had the opportunity of flying one. (See the photograph on p. 36.) Alternatively, by making a few minor alterations to the design you can change the theme to a more appropriate one for your child. For example, the kite could be replaced by a hot air balloon with basket, or even a small plastic plane (the sort you find in cheap party packs or under the counter of a toy shop). The design could even be changed completely to create a space theme. Darken the blue base colour and add small cut-out stars and a simple space shuttle. Coloured planets could then take the place of the hills and valleys around the base of the cake.

———

*1* Using a large knife halve the cake horizontally. Spread the buttercream over the lower half with a palette knife. Cover with the second cake half and place on the board.
*2* Melt the jam in a saucepan then press through a sieve. Brush over the top and sides of the cake. Using a cocktail stick, dot a little blue food colouring into 750 g (1 ½ lb) of the moulding icing and knead it. Colour another 50 g (2 oz) brown, 50 g (2 oz) bright green and 50 g (2 oz) dull green. (Add a little black or brown food colouring to the bright green if you don't have a separate green colouring.) From the remaining icing colour a small piece red and a small piece yellow, leaving the remainder white.
*3* Roll out the blue icing on a surface dusted with cornflour or icing sugar to a 28 cm (11 in) circle. Lift the icing over the cake and smooth over the top and sides using hands dusted with cornflour or icing sugar. Ease the icing around the sides, smoothing with the hands to eliminate any creases. Trim off the excess icing around the base.

4  Brush the board and lower edges of the cake with a little water. Roll out the bright green icing and cut out a large semi-circle. Position around the side of the cake, pressing icing around the bottom edges and letting the excess over-hang the edges of the board. Complete building up the sides of the cake with more pieces of green icing in both shades, and the brown icing. Vary the size of each piece cut (see drawing). Trim off the excess icing around the edges of the board.

5  Thinly roll out the red and yellow icing. Trace the kite template (see page 106) onto greaseproof or bakewell paper and cut out the 4 sections. Lay over the icing and cut out to give 2 red sections and 2 yellow. Secure to the top of the cake using a dampened paintbrush. Press the piece of liquorice into the cake for kite string. Make a few bows from the red icing trimmings and secure to the liquorice.

6  Thinly roll out the white icing and cut out a few clouds. Secure to the cake. Cut the dolly mixtures into smaller pieces and position in clusters around the base of the cake. Make small roofs from brown icing trimmings and press into position. Using black food colouring and a paint-brush, or an icing pen, paint small birds on the blue icing.

### EQUIPMENT

*Large sharp knife*
*Palette knife*
*28 cm (11 in) round silver*
  *cake board*
*Sieve*
*Pastry brush*
*Cocktail sticks*
*Rolling-pin*
*Paintbrush*
*Greaseproof or bakewell*
  *paper*

*Press the icing semi-circles around the bottom of the cake to create the hills and valleys.*

# WINTER WONDERLAND

## SERVES

—— 18-20 ——

### INGREDIENTS

23 cm (9 in) round
  Madeira cake (see p. 24)
  or Quick cake mix (see
  p. 22)
225 g (8 oz) Buttercream
  (see p. 42)
900 g (2 lb) Moulding
  icing (see p. 30)
Cornflour or icing sugar
  for dusting
20 white or silver wired
  paper leaves
White or silver candles
20 icing-dusted toffee
  bonbons
Silver dragées
Skis or other small motif
Caster sugar

This would make a pretty cake for a girl who has a birthday during the winter. It might also make a Christmas cake if you wanted something completely different. (See the photograph on p. 35.) The little skis are strips of cardboard, pointed and turned up at one end, then covered with kitchen foil. The ski sticks are from a small toy. Even if you can't get hold of these, toy shops or shops that sell Christmas decorations often have small ice skates or a silver sledge that would look equally effective. Cake decorating shops also have a range of 'wintery' decorations, such as the paper leaves, that you could arrange on top of the cake.

*Even out the folds of the icing with your fingers.*

1 Place the cake on the board. Using a palette knife, spread the buttercream evenly over the top and the sides.
2 Lightly brush the cake board with water. Roll out 225 g (8 oz) of the moulding icing on a surface dusted with cornflour or icing sugar. Use to cover the cake board, smoothing out any creases and joins using hands dusted with cornflour or icing sugar. Trim off the excess icing around the edges of the board.
3 Knead the trimmings into the remaining icing. Roll out to a 33 cm (13 in) circle and lift the icing over the cake. Let the icing fall down the sides of the cake in loose folds. Use the fingers to even out the folds where necessary (see drawing).
4 Trim the wire on the leaves down to about 2.5 cm (1 in). Arrange the leaves over and around the cake, just piercing the icing with the wire to secure, and twisting some wires together to make sprays.
5 Press the candles into the icing, some on the cake and some on the board. Press the bonbons in clusters onto and around the cake. Press the dragées into the icing around the bonbons.
6 Sprinkle the undecorated top surface of the cake with caster sugar and arrange the ski decoration. Using a cocktail stick, mark curved ski lines into the sugar.

### EQUIPMENT

*30 cm (12 in) round silver cake board*
*Palette knife*
*Pastry brush*
*Rolling-pin*
*Cocktail stick*

# PIRATE

### S E R V E S
#### — 8 —

**INGREDIENTS**

*15 cm (6 in) round tin
quantity of Moist
chocolate cake (see
p. 26), Madeira cake
(see p. 24) or Quick
cake mix (see p. 22)
Blue, brown, red and black
food colourings
900 g (2 lb) Moulding
icing (see p. 30)
Cornflour or icing sugar
for dusting
4 tablespoons apricot jam
10 liquorice 'bootlaces'
Eye patch
Earring
Pirate's hat*

This is one of the easiest novelty cakes to make as there's no delicate work involved in the decorating. In fact, the more slap-happy you are with the features, the more rough and ready the pirate will look. (See the photograph on p. 37.) Earrings and eye patches are available from toy or joke shops, or fancy dress hire shops. The cardboard hat is from a packet of children's party hats, although you could easily cut out the simple shape from a piece of coloured card.

The sponge cake is baked in a large 3.4 litre (6 pint) Pyrex bowl in order to get a shallow domed cake. If you don't have a bowl of this size, you can make or buy a 20–23 cm (8–9 in) round cake and round off the edges to give a shallow dome.

*1* Pre-heat the oven to gas mark 3, 325°F (160°C). Grease the mixing bowl then line the base with a circle of greaseproof paper (see p. 14). Grease the greaseproof. Turn the cake mixture into the bowl and level the surface. Bake for the time stated in recipe. Leave the cake to cool in the bowl, then remove and peel off the paper.
*2* Using a cocktail stick, dot some blue food colouring into 350 g (12 oz) of the moulding icing and knead in. Roll out on a surface dusted with cornflour or icing sugar to a 33 cm (13 in) circle. Lightly brush the cake board with water then lay the icing over the board. Smooth out gently with the palms of the hands then trim off excess around the edges.
*3* Place the cake on the board. Melt the jam in a saucepan then press through a sieve. Brush over the cake.
*4* Reserve 50 g (2 oz) of the moulding icing and colour the remainder pale brown. Mould a small piece into a pear shape and position just below the centre of the cake to shape the nose. Roll another small piece into a sausage, thinning out at the ends and secure to lower edge of the cake for chin.

5 Reserve a small piece of brown icing then roll out the remainder to a 25 cm (10 in) circle. Lay over the cake and smooth around the sides, fitting icing around the nose and chin (see drawing). Trim off the excess icing around the base of the cake. Indent the nostrils with the tip of a wooden spoon.

6 Divide the remaining brown icing in half. Press one piece against one side of the cake to make an ear. Press the other piece against the other side of the cake, tucking in the earring.

7 Scrunch the liquorice to curl it up then press around the cake for hair. Press the eye patch to one side of the nose. Roll a small piece of the remaining white icing, about the size of a grape, into an oval shape. Secure to the cake to make the other eye. Shape another small piece of white icing into a tooth. Divide the remaining white icing in half. Colour one half red and the other a darker shade of brown. Use a little of this brown icing to shape the centre of the eye.

8 Shape the remainder into a crooked mouth and secure in place. Add lips made from thin 'sausages' of red icing and position the tooth. Paint the centre of the eye with brown colouring.

9 Scrunch up a piece of kitchen paper and dot it with a little black food colouring. Gently dab the cake to create 'stubble'. Place the hat in position over the hair.

**EQUIPMENT**

*3.4 litre (6 pint) Pyrex mixing bowl*
*Cocktail sticks*
*Rolling-pin*
*Pastry brush*
*33 cm (13 in) round silver cake board*
*Sharp knife*
*Sieve*
*Wooden spoon*
*Paintbrush*
*Piece of kitchen paper or tissue*

*Lay the icing over the cake, fitting it around the nose and chin.*

# SUNFLOWER

### S E R V E S
—— 10–12 ——

**INGREDIENTS**

*18 cm (7 in) round Quick*
*cake mix (see p. 22),*
*Moist chocolate cake (see*
*p. 26) or Madeira cake*
*(see p. 24)*
*225 g (8 oz) Buttercream*
*(see p. 42)*
*Green, yellow and brown*
*food colourings*
*About 40 long flat fruit*
*chews*
*1 piece of coloured foil*
*1 oval sweet*
*Antennae*

Most cakes that display an abundance of flowers involve a complicated process of shaping individual petals and leaving them to harden before assembling them on the cake. This cake takes a time-saving shortcut with the use of fruit 'chew' sweets which are cut with scissors into petal shapes, then positioned on the cake. (See the photograph on p. 33.) You need the thin, bendy chews, about 7.5 cm (3 in) long and 1 cm (½ in) wide which are usually a pale yellow colour, regardless of flavour. Although the recipe uses 40 of them, they're often sold in net packs from stores with a large confectionery department.

For the butterfly's wings save a piece of coloured foil from a chocolate bar or biscuit wrapper. The body can be any oval shaped sweet – a jelly bean, sugared almond, or boiled sweet. And for the antennae there are various suitably shaped options. You can thread two small round sweets onto the end of two cocktail sticks. Large cake decorating stamens also work well or, if they're in season when you make the cake, cherry stalks look just right.

*Arrange the chews so that the outside tips slightly
extend over the edge of the cake.*

*1* Using a knife cut out a deep hollow from the centre of the cake to give a crater-like dip. Finish by scooping with a spoon to give curved sides. Place the cake on the board.

*2* Reserve 3 tablespoons of the buttercream. Using a cocktail stick, apply green colouring to the remainder and mix in. Using a palette knife spread the green icing all over the cake.

*3* Cut each fruit chew into a petal shape by cutting the flat ends into points using scissors. Arrange the chews over the top of the cake so that the outside tips slightly extend the edge of the cake (see drawing). Halve the remaining chews and make an inner circle of petals.

*4* Using the paintbrush, roughly paint the chews with yellow food colouring.

*5* Colour a third of the remaining 3 tablespoons of buttercream pale brown and the remaining two-thirds a darker shade of brown by adding extra food colouring. Fit the piping bag with the nozzle and spoon the pale buttercream into the bag. Press the icing down to the nozzle then open the bag and add the darker icing.

*6* Pipe circles of stars into the centre of the flower, starting at the edge and working inwards, so that the darker colour comes through as you get near the centre.

*7* Trace the 'wings' template (see page 107) onto greaseproof or bakewell paper and cut out. Lay the paper cut-out over the foil and cut around. Place the sweet in the centre and bend the foil wings round slightly. Position on the cake. Press the antennae into the cake, just in front of the sweet.

**EQUIPMENT**

*Sharp knife*
*23 cm (9 in) round gold or*
  *silver cake board*
*Cocktail sticks*
*Palette knife*
*Scissors*
*Paintbrush*
*Paper or nylon piping bag*
  *(see p. 15)*
*Medium star piping nozzle*
*Greaseproof or bakewell*
  *paper*

# CAKES FOR GROWN-UPS

With the sudden popularity of 'novelty' cakes, in which icing can be moulded into virtually any shape, celebration cakes for adults have taken on a new lease of life. We too can now enjoy the thrill of a surprise birthday cake, and giving one as a gift can come to the rescue when you're stuck for a good present idea. Everyone likes receiving a present that has had time and thought put into it, even if it stems from a quick and easy idea.

As is often the case with presents it's easier to think up ideas for women rather than men. Fresh or sugar-frosted flowers, prettily arranged on a cake with a wide ribbon around the sides, make an easy but attractive cake. Alternatively you can shape blossom flowers from icing with a small cutter and arrange randomly or in clusters over a cake (like the Pink tulle cake on p. 81).

Cakes for men will undoubtedly require more thought and this is where novelty ideas come in very useful. A particular aspect of a hobby or task they enjoy (or dislike!) whether it's gardening, DIY, sport, music or food can be recreated in cake form by first shaping the cake, then covering with moulding icing, and finally adding the details. You need no special equipment, other than what's already at hand in the average kitchen, and even the most basic range of colours can be used to the full by colour mixing (see opposite). For large quantities of icing in the same colour it's best to knead in the chosen colour. Details such as writing, patterns, features, etc., can be painted on using a fine paintbrush. Dilute the food colour with a little water if using a paste or concentrated liquid colour. Painting directly onto a cake cannot easily be erased so practise the colour shade and design on a spare rolled icing (or white paper if you've run out of icing) if you're unsure of how it's going to look.

Unless you're purposely building up an interesting selection of food colourings you won't want to spend a lot of money on different colours. Mixing a few basic ones in different proportions can give a surprising variety of colours and shades.

*Blue + Yellow = Green*

*Green + Yellow = Lime-green*

*Blue + Red = Purple, Burgundy, Lilac*

*Red + Yellow = Orange, Peach*

*Blue + Green = Turquoise*

*Red + Yellow = Light brown*

Use just a dash of red to give a pale pink or flesh colour. A dash of black produces a soft grey.

# MONEY MOUNTAIN

## SERVES
—— 16–18 ——

### INGREDIENTS

18 cm (7 in) round tin
  quantity of Rich or
  Light fruit cake (see
  pp. 18 and 20)
225 g (8 oz) white almond
  paste
Icing sugar for dusting
3 tablespoons apricot jam
450 g (1 lb) Royal icing
  (see p. 29) or
  Buttercream (see p. 42)
8 packets gold-wrapped
  chocolate coins
About 20 gold-wrapped
  rectangular chocolates

There may be years to run on the mortgage, that old banger may need repairing and those investments may be tied up for years – so why not give away a money mountain! Chocolate coins so evoke memories of childhood Christmases that the sight of all that gold should gild any celebration. Fortunately these coins are now available all year round and this easily made cake suits all ages and occasions. (See the photograph on p. 38.)

The cake is baked in a pudding basin and then covered with icing to make a convenient base for securing the chocolate. Use buttercream or, if the cake is to be stored for a while, a thin layer of royal icing.

*1* Pre-heat the oven to gas mark 1, 275°F (140°C).
*2* Grease the pudding basin then line the base with a circle of greaseproof paper (see p. 14). Grease the greaseproof. Turn the cake mixture into the basin and level the surface. Bake for the time stated in the recipe. Leave to cool in the basin, then remove and peel off the paper. Trim off the top of the cake if highly domed.
*3* Using a knife cut off the curved sides of the cake to leave a more cone-shaped cake. Slice the cake horizontally into three.
*4* Halve the almond paste. Roll one half out, on a surface dusted with icing sugar, to a circle about the diameter of the cake. Place the bottom cake layer on the cake board and cover with the circle of almond paste. Cover this with the middle cake layer. Roll out the remaining almond paste to a slightly smaller circle and position on the cake. Cover with the remaining cake (see drawing).
*5* Melt the jam in a saucepan then press through a sieve. Brush over the cake. Using a palette knife, cover the cake completely with the royal icing or buttercream.
*6* Starting at the bottom of the cake press the gold-wrapped chocolates gently into the icing. Gradually work up the sides of the cake overlapping the sweets so that barely any icing can be seen through the wrappings. Scatter any remaining chocolates over the cake board.

**EQUIPMENT**

*1.5 litre (2 ½ pint) pudding basin*
*Large sharp knife*
*Rolling-pin*
*28 cm (11 in) round gold cake board*
*Sieve*
*Pastry brush*
*Palette knife*

*Place the last piece of cake on top of the circle of almond paste.*

**69**

# FROSTED FRUIT AND FLOWERS CAKE

## SERVES

—— 18–20 ——

### INGREDIENTS

450 g (1 lb) mixture of fruits
1 egg white
Caster sugar
8–10 flowers
Petals of 1 small rose (optional)
23 cm (9 in) round Madeira cake (see p. 24) or Quick mix cake (see p. 22)
4 tablespoons Cointreau or Grand Marnier
4 tablespoons orange juice
225 g (8 oz) Buttercream (see p. 42)
225 g (8 oz) almond paste
Icing sugar for dusting
1 metre (3 feet) ribbon

Combining beautiful ingredients like fresh fruit and flowers takes you half-way to success without even trying. Here they're frosted with sugar and casually piled up on a buttercream and almond-pasted sponge to make a really colourful and pretty cake. (See the front cover photograph.) There are some limitations on which fruits and flowers you can use. The fruits must have a firm skin so that the sugar doesn't absorb the juices from the fruit and turn to a sticky syrup. For appearance's sake it is best to select small whole fruits like berries and grapes, as they're all frosted whole. The flowers must be non-poisonous with petals that can easily be reached with a fine brush. The choice of both fruit and flowers will change with the seasons and suitable choices are listed opposite.

If there's time, prepare the fruits and flowers the day before you need the cake as they'll be easier to arrange and remain crisp for longer. You really only need five minutes for the final assembly.

SPRING

*Flowers*
Primula
Primrose
Petunia
Violets
*Fruits*
Green grapes
Kumquats
Apricots
Gooseberries
Yellow ribbon

SUMMER

*Flowers*
Freesia
Pansies
Herb flowers
Rose petals
*Fruits*
Redcurrants
Blackcurrants
Cherries
Small peaches
or nectarines
Pink ribbon

AUTUMN

*Flowers*
Rose petals
*Fruits*
Yellow plums
Blackberries
Cape gooseberries
Blueberries
Orange ribbon

WINTER

*Flowers*
Rose petals
*Fruits*
Black grapes
Cranberries
Figs
Satsuma segments
Red or gold ribbon

EQUIPMENT

*Kitchen paper*
*Paintbrush*
*Wire cooling rack*
*Palette knife*
*String*
*Rolling-pin*
*Cocktail sticks*
*Serving plate*

*1* Wash the fruit only if necessary, and thoroughly dry on kitchen paper. Beat the egg white in a small bowl. Place the sugar in a separate bowl. Brush the fruit with egg white and then dredge with the sugar until completely coated. Transfer to the rack to dry. (For very small berries, place them on a sheet of foil.) Coat the flowers in the same way, brushing the petals on both sides before sprinkling with the sugar. Coat each rose petal separately (if using). Leave the fruits and flowers for several hours, or overnight, to dry.

*2* Place the cake on a serving plate. Mix the liqueur with the orange juice and drizzle over the cake. Using a palette knife, spread the top and sides of the cake with the buttercream.

*3* Measure the circumference of the cake with a length of string. Roll out the almond paste on a surface dusted with icing sugar to a long strip the length of the string and 7.5 cm (3 in) wide.

*4* Dust several cocktail sticks with icing sugar, then press them, 1 cm (½ in) apart, down the strip. Gently roll over the sticks with the rolling-pin so that they are pressed into the paste. Remove the sticks to leave decorative lines. Repeat the decoration all the way down the strip (see drawing).

*5* Arrange the almond paste strip around the cake, pressing gently against the buttercream.

*6* Arrange the fruits and flowers attractively over the top of the cake, piling up slightly in the centre. Tie the ribbon around the cake.

*Place cocktail sticks 1cm (½ in) apart on the strip of almond paste and gently roll over them to make the decorative lines.*

CHOCOLATE ROSE CAKE
*(see page 88)*

CHOCOLATE BAR
(*see page 90*)

CHOCOLATE PARCEL
(*see page 92*)

WHITE CHOCOLATE GÂTEAU
(*see page 94*)

BOWS AND GARLANDS CAKE
(*see page 97*)

HALLOWE'EN CAKE
(*see page 100*)

CHRISTMAS CAKE
(*see page 102*)

EASTER CAKE
(*see page 104*)

# PINK TULLE CAKE

### S E R V E S
#### — 20–24 —

This cake displays all the prettiness of a traditional, delicately iced cake, but involves a fraction of the effort. Small bundles of sugared almonds are wrapped in squares of tulle, tied with ribbon, and arranged around the cake. Further squares of tulle are tucked around the candles to soften the edges – and it's all done in a matter of minutes. (See the photograph on p. 39.)

To complete the cake, cut-out flowers are scattered around the board and on top of the cake. This is done with a small flower or blossom cutter, which is always a useful asset in the most basic cake decorating tool-box (see p. 12).

Tulle is available from both cake decorating shops and haberdashery departments of large stores. Alternatively you can use a fine, lacy fabric. If the cake is to be transported, secure the tulle bundles to the board with dots of dampened icing trimmings or scatter them around the board once the cake is finally positioned.

## INGREDIENTS

*23 cm (9 in) square
Madeira cake (see p. 24)
or Quick cake mix (see
p. 22)*
*8 tablespoons strawberry or
raspberry jam
225 g (8 oz) Buttercream
(see p. 42)
Pink food colouring
900 g (2 lb) Moulding
icing (see p. 30)
Cornflour or icing sugar
for dusting
1 metre (3 ¼ feet) pink
ribbon, about 4 cm
(1 ½ in) wide
Tall pink or white candles
50 cm (1 ¾ feet) white tulle
About 16 pink or white
sugared almonds
2 metres (6 ½ feet) pink
ribbon, about 5 mm
(¼ in) wide*

1 Mark the cake 5 cm (2 in) along the sides from one corner by pressing cocktail sticks into the cake. Using a knife, cut through the cake at the marked points to remove the corner. Repeat on the 3 remaining corners of the cake, using the first corner piece cut as a guide (see drawing).

2 Then cut the cake horizontally in half. Sandwich the cake together with 6 tablespoons of the jam, and the buttercream.

3 Knead pink food colouring into 225 g (8 oz) of the moulding icing until it is quite deeply coloured. Roll out on a surface dusted with cornflour or icing sugar to a 30 cm (12 in) square. Lightly brush the cake board with water to moisten then lay the icing over the board. Smooth out gently with the palms of the hands then trim off the excess around the sides of the board.

4 Place the cake on the board. Melt the remaining jam and press through a sieve. Brush over the top and sides of the cake.

5 Reserve 25 g (1 oz) of the remaining white moulding icing. Knead pink food colouring into the remaining icing until streaked with colour. Roll out the pink icing on a surface dusted with cornflour or icing sugar to a 35 cm (14 in) square. Lift the icing over the cake and smooth over the top and sides using hands dusted with cornflour or icing sugar. Ease the icing around the sides, smoothing with the hands to eliminate any creases. Trim off the excess icing around the base of the cake.

6 Tie the wide ribbon around the cake, securing the ends together with a dot of dampened icing.

7 Roll the deep pink icing trimmings into balls, each about the size of a small grape and press a candle into each. Press into position on the board, securing the bases using a dampened paintbrush.

*8* Cut the tulle into 11.5 cm (4½ in) squares. Place 2 sugared almonds in the centre of 8 pieces and tie into bundles with the thin ribbon. Scatter around the cake. Pinch the remaining tulle squares in the centre and twist slightly to secure in bundles then tuck them around the candles so that they remain bunched.

*9* Thinly roll out the reserved white icing on a surface dusted with cornflour or icing sugar and cut out small shapes with the cutter. Push the end of a paintbrush or pencil into the centre of the flower so that the petals curve up slightly. Secure the flowers to the cake with a dampened paintbrush. You'll need about 18 altogether.

**EQUIPMENT**

*Cocktail sticks*
*Large sharp knife*
*Palette knife*
*Rolling-pin*
*Pastry brush*
*30 cm (12 in) square silver*
  *cake board*
*Sieve*
*Paintbrush*
*Small flower or blossom*
  *cutter*

*Cut off the corners of the cake by measuring the first corner and then using it as a guide for the others.*

# ANCIENT RUIN

SERVES

—— 20 ——

25 cm (10 in) square
    Madeira cake (see p. 24)
1.5 kg (3 lb) Moulding
    icing (see p. 30)
Black, brown and green
    food colourings
Cornflour or icing sugar
    for dusting
4 tablespoons apricot jam
6 hexagonal, round or
    square cake pillars

With a little stretch of the imagination, plaster of Paris cake pillars bear a vague resemblance to the pillars of an ancient Greek monument. Broken, chipped, greyed with food colouring and haphazardly arranged on a similarly grey cake they begin to look really effective. (See the photograph on p. 40.) I have a collection of tattered cake pillars which serve the purpose perfectly, but a kitchen store or cake decorating shop might have a few damaged pillars that they'll sell off cheap. Otherwise it's simply a case of 'ruining' new pillars.

This cake would make an ideal present for a friend of 30, 40 or 50-ish, but perhaps not for anyone too much older – unless they've a good sense of humour!

1  Using a large, sharp knife cut several irregular steps from the cake, then cut a thin slice off the top of the cake if it is slightly domed (see drawing).
2  Using a cocktail stick dot 450 g (1 lb) of the moulding icing with plenty of black and brown food colourings. Roughly knead the colourings in on a surface dusted with icing sugar so that the icing is marbled and dark in colour. To make long streaks of colour roll the icing under the palms of the hands into a thick sausage then bend in the ends and re-roll.
3  Reserve 175 g (6 oz) of the coloured icing. Lightly brush the cake board with water to moisten. Thinly roll out the remaining coloured icing on a surface dusted with cornflour or icing sugar and lay it over the board. Smooth down lightly with the palms of the hands then trim off the excess icing.
4  Place the cake on the board. Melt the jam in a saucepan then press through a sieve. Use to completely cover the cake.

5  Knead a small amount of black and brown food colour-ings into the remaining moulding icing. Use much less colour and, again, only roughly knead it in. Roll out the icing and lift over the cake pressing the icing into the corners to emphasize the steps. Trim away the excess icing around the base of the cake. Using the back of a knife mark each tier of the cake into blocks. On one or two corners cut right through the step and pull away a section of the cake. Cover the exposed cake with thinly rolled pieces of the trimmed off icing. Cut a piece of cake off one of the top corners and lay it on a lower step. Cover the exposed cake with more icing.

6  Roll out the pale icing trimmings and cut out 2 semi-circles, one smaller than the other. Secure the larger circle against one step of the cake, then secure the smaller piece to this.

7  Use a knife and rolling-pin to cut through 2 of the cake pillars. Chip off more of the pillars at top and base. Arrange the pillars over the cake, moistening the icing with a dampened paintbrush to secure them, and pressing gently into the icing.

8  Dilute a little brown food colouring with water and brush over the pillars and in the knife marks made in the cake to give a weathered effect.

9  Roughly shape the reserved dark icing into rocks of varying sizes and arrange around the lower steps of the cake.

10  Using green food colouring and a fine paintbrush paint tufts of grass around the rocks.

## EQUIPMENT

*Large sharp knife*
*Cocktail sticks*
*Pastry brush*
*33 cm (13 in) square silver*
  *cake board*
*Rolling-pin*
*Small sharp knife*
*Sieve*
*Paintbrush*

*Cut several irregular steps from the cake and if it is slightly domed, a thin slice off the top.*

# CHOCOLATE CAKES

Almost everyone likes chocolate, so if you're making a cake for a birthday, special celebration, or to serve at a festive meal you can feel quite confident that it'll be highly popular. There are hundreds of different types of chocolate cakes, icings and decorative design ideas, from simple buttercream cakes to elaborate piped creations. The cakes in this chapter are not only quick and easy but also fun to make. The cakes themselves are made using the Moist chocolate cake recipe on p. 26. This is rich and chocolatey and can be made extra moist by drizzling with brandy, rum or an orange-flavoured liqueur. The White chocolate gâteau on p. 94 is soaked quite generously in an Amaretto syrup before decoration. This tastes excellent and gives the cake a very moist texture, perfect for a dessert if served with pouring cream.

I've included some icings and pastes which are really enjoyable to use. Chocolate ganache (see p. 41) has a delicious truffle-like taste, while Chocolate modelling paste (see p. 44) can be shaped with almost as much versatility as ordinary moulding icing. Bearing in mind that white chocolate can be substituted for plain or milk, and vice versa, chocolate can give us plenty of inspiration for cake decorating.

Supermarkets, confectioners and cake decorating shops supply a wide variety of chocolate. These are briefly explained in the Store-cupboard chapter (pp. 8–11). Plain, milk or white chocolate can be used successfully in most icings although plain chocolate is generally easier to work with because of its silky, smooth texture. It's also less likely to overheat when used in cooking.

There's little that can go wrong when using chocolate provided the chocolate is melted correctly. To do this, break the chocolate into a heatproof bowl and place it over a pan of hot, but not boiling, water. The bowl should not touch the water as this will overheat the chocolate. Leave, without stirring, until the chocolate has completely melted. Once melted, stir the chocolate very gently until smooth. Lift away from the heat, making sure that no droplets of steam get into the bowl.

Chocolate can also be melted quickly in the microwave. Again, break the chocolate into pieces and place in a bowl. Microwave on a medium setting, allowing 2 minutes for 100 g (4 oz) of chocolate. Leave to stand for 2 minutes then stir gently. If still lumpy microwave for a little longer.

# CHOCOLATE ROSE CAKE

### S E R V E S
### —— 16 ——

*23 cm (9 in) round Moist
chocolate cake (see
p. 26), made using
20 cm (8 in) round
quantities*
*Chocolate ganache (see
p. 41)*
*Chocolate modelling paste
(see p. 44)*
*Several rose leaves*
*Icing sugar and cocoa
powder for dusting*

This cake illustrates how easy it is to imitate that continental *pâtisserie* look. A moist chocolate sponge is covered with Chocolate ganache and finished with simple decorations made from Chocolate modelling paste. The decorative roses are a short-cut version of the classic moulded rose. Instead of making up roses comprising separate petals, these are simply made by loosely rolling strips of paste. The results are fast and effective. (See the photograph on p. 73.)

The shallow depth of the cake is achieved by baking a 20 cm (8 in) round cake quantity in a 23 cm (9 in) tin, but if you prefer a deeper cake keep to the proper tin size. A white chocolate variation would look equally stunning; simply substitute white chocolate for the plain in both ganache and modelling paste and lightly dust with cocoa powder instead of icing sugar.

*Press a small ball of modelling paste onto the
underside of a rose leaf to make the decorative leaves.*

*1* Place the cake on the cooling rack over a large plate or tray to catch any drips. When the chocolate ganache has cooled enough to coat very thickly the back of a wooden spoon, pour it onto the surface of the cake and spread around the sides using a palette knife. Transfer the cake to a large flat plate.

*2* Take a small piece of the modelling paste, about the size of a large grape, and roll it as thinly as possible into a round. (You may need a dusting of icing sugar to prevent the paste sticking to the surface and rolling-pin, but avoid using too much.)

*3* Cut the circle in half. Press the curved edges of the semi-circle between thumbs and forefingers to give a slightly wavy edge. Position a semi-circle around the side of the cake so that the straight edge rests on the plate. Make and position more to complete the sides of the cake.

*4* To make a rose, take a small piece of paste and thinly roll to make a strip about 2 cm (¾ in) wide and 7.5 cm (3 in) long. Loosely roll up the strip to create a simple rose. Make more roses if you wish.

*5* To make leaves, take a small ball of modelling paste and press onto the underside of a rose leaf (see drawing). When peeled off the veining will show clearly on the chocolate. Make several more leaves in the same way. Make a small arrangement of small roses and leaves on top of the cake. Using a fine sieve or tea strainer lightly dust over the edges of the cake and the rose arrangement with icing sugar and cocoa powder.

**EQUIPMENT**

*Wire cooling rack*
*Wooden spoon*
*Palette knife*
*Rolling-pin*
*Sharp knife*
*Fine sieve or tea strainer*
*Large flat plate*

# CHOCOLATE BAR

### SERVES

—— 16 ——

20 cm (8 in) round tin
quantity of Moist
chocolate cake (see
p. 26)
175 g (6 oz) plain
chocolate
2 tablespoons liquid glucose
or golden syrup
1 egg white
450 g (1 lb) icing sugar
Red food colouring
225 g (8 oz) Moulding
icing (see p. 30)
Extra icing sugar for
dusting
1 tablespoon bought
chocolate pouring syrup
or a tube of writing
icing (see p. 11)

This is another cake that will suit just about anyone who loves chocolate. (See the photograph on p. 74.) The base is the Moist chocolate cake mixture baked in a shallow rectangular tin. Squares are cut from one end and then the whole cake is covered with a smooth chocolate icing. If you don't have the correct tin size, bake the cake in a 15–18 cm (6–7 in) square tin. Once cooled, split the cake horizontally then lay the halves side by side to shape the rectangle.

The red 'wrapping' is made using a small amount of moulding icing. To save time, buy a small packet of ready-made icing, or a larger one if you want to cover the board first. To avoid buying gold foil, which adds the finishing touches, save the gold wrapping from the chocolate bar used in the cake or icing. Finally, to complete the cake, the recipient's name can be written in chocolate syrup on the icing. Leave this part out if you don't trust your handwriting.

*Lay the chocolate icing over the cake, easing it around the sides and into the grooves.*

1 Grease the tin and line with greaseproof paper (see p. 14). Grease the paper. Turn the prepared mixture into the tin and level the surface. Bake for the time stated in the recipe then turn out onto a wire rack and leave to cool. Trim off any excess dome on top of the cake so that the cake sits flat when inverted onto a surface.

2 Using a sharp knife cut a 5 cm (2 in) slice off one end of the cake. Cut this slice into 3 squares. From the trimmed end of the large cake, cut out deep grooves to resemble squares of chocolate. Place the cake on the board with one of the cut-off squares resting against the large cake and the remaining 2 squares positioned randomly on the board.

3 Break up the chocolate and place in a bowl with the liquid glucose or golden syrup. Rest the bowl over a pan of gently simmering water and leave until melted, stirring occasionally until smooth. Remove from the heat. Leave for 2 minutes then add the egg white and a little of the icing sugar. Beat well until smooth, gradually adding the remaining sugar until too stiff to beat. Turn mixture out onto the surface and knead in the remaining icing sugar.

4 Roll out the chocolate icing and lay over the cake (see drawing). Ease the icing around the sides using hands dusted with icing sugar. Press the icing into the grooves made in cake. Trim off the excess icing and use this to cover the 2 small cakes.

5 Smooth out the gold wrapping. Use a little to cover the uncut end of the cake. Tuck 'torn off' bits around the other end of the cake.

6 Knead a little red food colouring into the moulding icing, then roll out thinly on a surface dusted with icing sugar. Lay over the cake so that the edges just cover the gold paper. Trim off excess around the sides of the cake. If using, place the chocolate syrup in the piping bag and snip off the smallest tip from the end. Use to pipe decorative lines over the red icing. Alternatively use the tube of writing icing. If liked, finish with the recipient's name.

**EQUIPMENT**

*28 × 18 × 4 cm*
*(11 × 7 × 1½ in)*
*shallow baking tin*
*Wiring cooling rack*
*Sharp knife*
*30–33 cm (12–13 in)*
*square silver cake board*
*Rolling-pin*
*Gold wrapping foil*
*Paper piping bag (see*
*p. 15)*

# CHOCOLATE PARCEL

### SERVES

—— 16 ——

**INGREDIENTS**

*Two 15 cm (6 in) Moist*
*chocolate cakes (see*
*p. 26)*
*450 g (1 lb) Chocolate-*
*flavoured buttercream*
*(see p. 42–3)*
*1 quantity each of white*
*and plain Chocolate*
*modelling paste (see*
*p. 44)*
*Icing sugar for dusting*

To achieve the depth that makes this cake so impress-
ive, it's best to stack two small 15 cm (6 in) round
chocolate cakes. Unless you have the time to bake two
cakes yourself, use good quality bought ones. (If they're
very shallow you may even need three.) Either bought or
home-made cakes can be drizzled with brandy or rum
before assembling so that they're really moist to eat. This
recipe uses chocolate-flavoured buttercream to sandwich
and cover the cakes, but whipped fresh cream would
make an equally delicious alternative.

If you have any modelling paste left after decorating
the cake, use it to cover the cake board. (See the photograph on p. 75.)

1 Using a sharp knife cut off any excess dome from the
tops of the cakes. Cut each cake horizontally in half. Place
one of the cake layers on the cake board and spread with a
little of the buttercream.
2 Cover with another cake layer and more buttercream.
Continue layering with more buttercream and cake.
Using a palette knife spread the remaining buttercream
over the top and sides of the cake until evenly covered.
3 Roll out half of the dark chocolate modelling paste, on

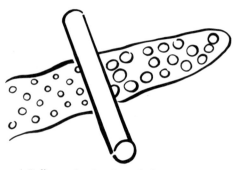

*1 Roll over the tiny dots of white modelling*
*icing to flatten them.*

a surface dusted with icing sugar, to a long thin strip about 40 cm (16 in) long and 6 cm (2½ in) wide. Roll tiny dots of the white modelling paste and arrange them over the plain chocolate strip. Lightly dust the rolling-pin with icing sugar and roll over the strip so that the white dots are flattened (see drawing 1).

4  Cut out 2 long thin strips from this paste, each about 3 cm (1¼ in) wide. Then cut the paste widthways to make 4 strips, each about 19 cm (7½ in) long. Reserve the trimmings of the strips to make the ribbon curls.

5  Brush the undersides of the spotted strips lightly with water then secure to the cake so that the ends come up over the top and almost meet in the centre of the cake.

6  Roll out the remaining dark chocolate modelling paste to a strip about 40 cm (16 in) long and 6 cm (2½ in) wide. Roll out a thin strip of white chocolate modelling paste, about the same length and 2.5 cm (1 in) wide. Cut this into thin ribbons and lay over the dark chocolate. Roll with a dusted rolling-pin until the white paste is secured to the dark. Cut into strips as with the spotted ribbon and use to decorate the cake in the same way.

7  Roll out the remaining white paste and use to make plain strips of paste to fill in any gaps around the cake.

8  Bend some of the ribbon trimmings, pinching ends to make loops to decorate the top of the cake (see drawing 2). Use some trimmings, unlooped, for ribbon ends.

### EQUIPMENT

*Sharp knife*
*Palette knife*
*23 cm (9 in) round silver cake board*
*Rolling-pin*
*Pastry brush*

*2 Decorate the cake with loops made from the ribbon trimmings.*

# *W*HITE CHOCOLATE GÂTEAU

## S E R V E S
—— 20 ——

INGREDIENTS

*23 cm (9 in) round Moist chocolate cake (see p. 26)*
*50 g (2 oz) caster sugar*
*75 ml (3 fl oz) water*
*4–5 tablespoons Amaretto or brandy*
*225 g (8 oz) Easy praline buttercream (see p. 42–3)*
*300 g (11 oz) white chocolate*
*Small posy of fresh flowers, tied with ribbon*

Τhis white chocolate decoration hides an almondy buttercream and rich chocolate cake, drizzled lavishly with almond syrup. Not only is the chocolate work easy, the cake is finished with one of the easiest decorations of all – a small posy of fresh flowers, tied with ribbon and laid on the surface of the cake. This always looks effective and the choice of flower can blend prettily with the creamy colour of the chocolate or contrast with bolder shades. (See the photograph on p. 76.) If you're a devoted fan of dark chocolate, use it in place of the white for the decoration.

*1 Lift the greaseproof paper at the edges and shake it gently to make the chocolate completely smooth.*

*1* Place the cake on a large flat plate and pierce the surface with the small skewer. Place the sugar and water in a small pan and heat gently, stirring until the sugar dissolves. Bring to the boil and boil for 1 minute. Remove from the heat and stir in the Amaretto or brandy. Spoon over the cake until it is absorbed.

*2* Using a palette knife spread the buttercream all over the top and sides of the cake, spreading as evenly as possible.

*3* Break up the chocolate into a bowl. Stand the bowl over a saucepan of gently simmering water and leave until melted. Remove from the heat and stir gently.

*4* Cut out a circle of greaseproof paper, 38 cm (15 in) in diameter. Using a palette knife, spread the melted chocolate in a thin even layer over the paper, almost to the edges. To help make the chocolate completely smooth lift up the paper at the edges and shake it gently (see drawing 1).

*5* When the chocolate has firmed up slightly and is no longer runny, invert it onto the cake so that the chocolate is face down and the chocolate-covered paper falls in soft folds around the cake. Arrange the folds around the sides of the cake so that they fall evenly. Place the cake in the refrigerator for 30 minutes to allow the chocolate to set.

*6* Starting around the base of the cake, slowly peel off the greaseproof paper (see drawing 2).

*7* Arrange a posy of flowers on top of the cake just before serving.

**EQUIPMENT**

*Large flat plate*
*Small skewer*
*Palette knife*
*Extra wide greaseproof*
*  paper*
*Fine sieve or tea strainer*

*2 Slowly peel off the greaseproof paper, starting at the base of the cake.*

# SPECIAL OCCASIONS

There are certain occasions throughout the year when a cake is almost compulsory. Fortunately the choice of cake and its decoration is much more flexible today. For example, you no longer need to spend a fortune on ordering a classic white wedding cake with lots of elaborate piping. Instead you can have a simple, pretty cake in fruit, chocolate or Madeira – or combine tiers of different flavours so that everyone gets a taste of what they like, and the cake won't be left hanging around for months after the event.

Although this is a relatively short chapter to incorporate so many special occasions that might take place during the year, two of the cakes are flexible in their usage. The pretty, tiered cake on p. 97 is ideal for any anniversary, or 'big' birthday, while the Easter cake would serve equally well as a gift for Mother's Day. If the same cake was made in a heart-shaped tin, it would also make a good choice for a Valentine's Day cake. You can even seek inspiration from some of the other chapters for a special celebration. How about a huge Chocolate bar cake (p. 90) or a Surprise parcel (p. 56) for a friend's retirement. By incorporating a decorative key to the Pink tulle cake on p. 81 you have a smart cake for an 18th or 21st birthday celebration.

The following cakes are all designed with the busy party planner in mind. The sponge or fruit base can be made well in advance and tightly wrapped, or frozen, ready to decorate when you have the time. Even the tiered cake can be decorated in a couple of hours, and will sit quite happily for a week or two if you want to get it made well before the party. Once hardened, cover it loosely with cling film and put in a box in a cool, dry place.

# BOWS AND GARLANDS CAKE

### S E R V E S
### —— 45 ——

This really is a cake that anyone can make, whether it's for an informal wedding, christening, anniversary or simply a stunning centrepiece for a summer celebration in the garden. (See the photograph on p. 77.) The design is simple, yet effective, and offers plenty of scope for variations. Colour can be added by making the bows and garlands in coloured icing. For a silver wedding anniversary, fine silver ribbon can be laid over the garland strips before shaping and then twisted in. The same could be done for a golden anniversary. Deep red decorations would be perfect for a ruby celebration while soft pastels would make a pretty christening variation.

The design does away with the worry of cake pillars by stacking one tier directly over another. This makes assembly much easier and the tiers are simply cut from the top downwards instead of the other way round. There's also no piping to do at all – instead fine haberdashery beading is positioned around the base of each tier. The number of tiers is also flexible – it can be reduced to one or raised to three (for this a 30 cm/12 in bottom tier would be ideal). The recipe uses rich fruit cake in traditional style, but this can be changed to light fruit, Madeira or moist chocolate if preferred, bearing in mind that these won't serve as many.

*15 cm (6 in) and 23 cm
(9 in) Rich fruit cakes
(see p. 18)
6 tablespoons apricot jam
1.5 kg (3 lb) almond paste
1.75 kg (4 lb) Moulding
icing (see p. 30)
Cornflour or icing sugar
for dusting
2 metres (6½ feet) fine
white beading
Posy of fresh flowers*

1 Place the large cake on the cake board and the small cake on a plate. Melt the jam in a small saucepan then press through a sieve. Brush over the cakes.

2 Roll out 225 g (8 oz) of the almond paste, on a surface dusted with icing sugar, to a circle the same as the diameter of the small cake. (Use the cake tin as a guide.) Lay the paste over the top of the cake, pressing the paste around the top edge with a palette knife to neaten.

3 Measure the circumference and depth of the cake with 2 lengths of string. Roll out another 350 g (12 oz) of the paste to a strip long enough to go around the sides of the cake, using the pieces of string as a guide. Press the paste into position around the sides of the cake.

4 Cover the larger cake in the same way, allowing 350 g (12 oz) of paste for the top and the remaining 450 g (1 lb) for the sides.

5 Roll out 900 g (2 lb) of the moulding icing, on a surface dusted with cornflour or icing sugar, to a 30 cm (12 in) circle. Lift the icing over the large cake and smooth over the top and sides using hands dusted with cornflour or icing sugar. Ease the icing around the sides, smoothing with the hands to eliminate any creases. Trim off the excess icing around the base of the cake.

6 Use another 750 g (1½ lb) of the moulding icing to cover the small cake in the same way. Using a fish slice to lift the cake, position the small cake centrally over the large cake.

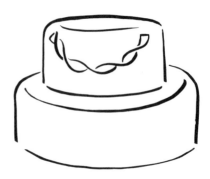

*1 Gently twist the strip of icing and secure the ends
to the cake beneath the pin marks.*

7 Cut a strip of greaseproof paper, the circumference and depth of the small cake (use the string as a guide). Fold the paper in half, then in half again to give 4 thicknesses. Unfold the paper and wrap around the sides of the small cake, securing ends with dressmaker's pins. Using a cocktail stick make a mark into the icing at the top of each crease line and where the 2 ends of paper join. Use the same technique on the large cake, but fold the paper strip into 6 thicknesses.

8 Roll out a little of the remaining moulding icing and cut out 4 strips, each 14 cm (5 ½ in) long and 5 mm (¼ in) wide. Lightly dampen the cake just below 2 neighbouring cocktail stick marks on the small cake. Gently twist one of the strips between the fingers then secure to the cake so that the ends just meet the pin marks. Make 3 more twists around the small cake (see drawing 1).

9 Make twists around the large cake in the same way.

10 Cut another strip of icing 13 cm (5 in) long and 5 mm (¼ in) wide. Lightly dampen the surface with a paintbrush. Fold both the ends so that they cross over in the centre then pinch through the centre of all thickness with the forefingers to make a simple bow (see drawing 2). Lightly dampen the back and secure the bow at the point where 2 twists meet. Make and secure more bows in the same way.

11 Place the beading around the bottom of each tier, pressing gently into the icing to secure.

12 Arrange a posy of flowers on top of the cake.

## EQUIPMENT

*28 cm (11 in) round silver cake board*
*Sieve*
*Pastry brush*
*Rolling-pin*
*Palette knife*
*String*
*Small sharp knife*
*Fish slice*
*Greaseproof paper*
*Dressmaker's pins*
*Cocktail sticks*
*Paintbrush*

*2 To make a bow, fold over a lightly dampened strip of icing and pinch through the centre.*

# HALLOWE'EN CAKE

### SERVES

—— 16 ——

**INGREDIENTS**

*20 cm (8 in) round tin
quantity of Madeira
cake (see p. 24)
8 tablespoons apricot jam
225 g (8 oz) Buttercream
(see p. 42)
900 g (2 lb) Moulding
icing (see p. 30)
Orange and blue food
colourings
Cornflour or icing sugar
for dusting
12 black, blue or orange
candles*

With its richly contrasting colours and ring of candles, this cake makes an eye catching centre-piece for a Hallowe'en feast. (See the photograph on p. 78.) If you want to have the candles lit for more than the duration of the average cake candle then substitute night lights and use a slightly larger cake board. The idea might also be adapted to a Fireworks' Night cake by replacing some of the stars and crescents with swirls, splashes and streaks of colour, representing exploding fireworks.

When icing needs to be very darkly coloured, it can sometimes absorb quite a lot of colouring and take a surprisingly long time to knead in. It can also leave everyone who eats the cake with an equally colourful tongue. For this reason the colour has been painted onto the icing. Applied with a large pastry brush and slightly diluted blue colouring, this takes just a couple of minutes.

If you don't have the star and crescent cutters improvize so that you don't have to buy any. The crescent shapes can be made by cutting out overlapping circles using a round-shaped cutter. For the stars cut out small star shapes from cardboard. Rest them over the rolled icing and cut around with a pointed knife.

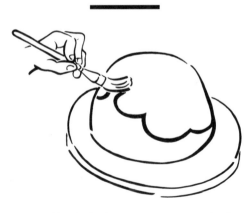

*Paint on blue food colouring to create the night sky.*

1 Pre-heat the oven to gas mark 3, 325°F (160°C). Grease the pudding basin or mixing bowl then line the base with a circle of greaseproof paper (see p. 14). Grease the greaseproof. Turn the cake mixture into the basin and level the surface. Bake for the time stated in the recipe. Leave to cool in the basin, then remove and peel off the paper. Cut off any dome on the cake so that it sits flat when inverted onto a surface. Slice the cake horizontally into 3 layers.

2 Place the largest cake layer on the cake board and spread with 3 tablespoons of the jam. Cover with half the buttercream, then place the middle section of the cake on top of this. Spread this with another 3 tablespoons of the jam and the remaining buttercream. Cover with the remaining cake section.

3 Melt the remaining jam in a saucepan then press through a sieve. Brush over the cake.

4 Reserve 50 g (2 oz) of the moulding icing. Using a cocktail stick to apply the colouring, colour 225 g (8 oz) with orange and then roll out the remaining, on a surface dusted with cornflour or icing sugar, to a 33 cm (13 in) circle. Lay over the cake and smooth over the top and sides using hands dusted with cornflour or icing sugar. Ease the icing around the sides, smoothing with the hands to eliminate any creases. Trim off the excess around the base of the cake.

5 Using blue food colouring and a pastry brush, swirl the colour onto the icing until completely covered (see drawing).

6 Thinly roll out all but 50 g (2 oz) of the orange icing to a long strip, about 35 cm (14 in) long and 13 cm (5 in) wide. Cut in half lengthways. Lightly dampen the cake board then lay one strip around the board, fitting the cut edge against the base of the cake. Arrange the other strip to cover the remaining board. Smooth out the joins then trim off excess icing around the edges of the board.

7 Roll out the remaining orange and reserved white icing and cut out star and crescent shapes. Arrange over the cake. Re-roll icing trimmings and cut out more stars. Secure these to the iced board using a dampened brush. Press a candle into the centre of each.

**EQUIPMENT**

*2.25 litre (4 pint) pudding basin or mixing bowl*
*Large sharp knife*
*33 cm (13 in) round silver cake board*
*Palette knife*
*Sieve*
*Pastry brush*
*Cocktail sticks*
*Rolling-pin*
*Small star and crescent cutters*

# CHRISTMAS CAKE

S E R V E S

—— 20–24 ——

## INGREDIENTS

*18 cm (7 in) square Rich
or Light fruit cake (see
pp. 18 and 20)
4 tablespoons apricot jam
900 g (2 lb) almond paste
900 g (2 lb) Moulding
icing (see p. 30)
Red and green food
colourings
Cornflour or icing sugar
for dusting
10–12 red candles
A few Christmas
decorations (e.g. holly,
ribbon, fir cones)*

From the conventional 'snow' theme and holly leaves to pretty parcel cakes with seasonal trimmings there are many quick and easy ways to decorate a Christmas cake. The following cake is equally easy, makes an attractive centrepiece and, because of its shape, is totally out of the ordinary. (See the photograph on p. 79.)

If you want the candles to be lit for some time don't choose ordinary cake candles which burn down very quickly. Instead buy the slightly larger, sturdier candles that are often used on small table decorations. These can be pressed directly into the icing or into candle holders depending on personal preference. However you assemble the candles, don't leave the room unattended when they're lit.

The cake is finished with a selection of Christmas decorations like fir cones, bows and a sprig of holly. These are best kept to a minimum to avoid detracting from the simplicity of the cake.

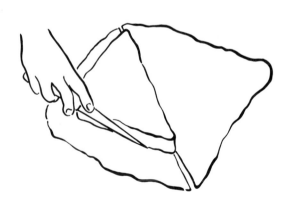

*Cut out the almond paste around the cake.*

*1* Using a sharp knife, cut the cake in half diagonally. Arrange the cake sections side by side to create a triangle. Melt the jam in a small saucepan, then press through a sieve. Brush a little over the 2 cake sides that join together, then re-join them. Stand the cake upright and brush over all the sides with the remaining jam.

*2* Roll out the almond paste, on a surface dusted with icing sugar, to a 30 cm (12 in) square. Lay the cake diagonally over half the paste, then cut around the cake, through the paste (see drawing). Flip the cake onto the remaining paste and cut around in the same way. Position the cake diagonally on the board.

*3* Re-roll the almond paste trimming to a long thin strip and use to cover the 2 sloping sides of the cake. Colour the reserved icing green.

*4* Reserve 100 g (4 oz) of the moulding icing and, using a cocktail stick to apply colouring, colour the remainder red. Roll out the red icing, on a surface dusted with cornflour or icing sugar, to a 28 cm (11 in) square then cut diagonally in half.

*5* Dampen the almond paste with a little water. Lift and position one of the pieces of red icing against one side of the cake. Smooth against the cake using hands dusted with cornflour or icing sugar until the icing is firmly in position. Trim off excess paste on all sides. Fit the remaining red icing to the other side of the cake, smoothing to fit and trimming off excess.

*6* Re-roll the red trimmings and cut out a long thin strip. Use to cover the 2 sloping sides of the cake. Colour the reserved icing green.

*7* Roll out the green icing to a strip 28 cm (11 in) long and 5 cm (2 in) wide. Cut into 4 thin strips. Dampen the sloping edges of the cake with water then secure a green strip to each, trimming off ends neatly. Press a candle into the top of the cake, then space more candles evenly down the sides. Press any remaining candles into small balls of red icing trimmings and secure to the cake board. Decorate with ribbon, fir cones and holly leaves.

**EQUIPMENT**

*Large sharp knife*
*Sieve*
*Pastry brush*
*Rolling-pin*
*30 cm (12 in) square gold cake board*
*Cocktail sticks*

**103**

# E ASTER CAKE

S E R V E S

—— 20-24 ——

**INGREDIENTS**

Oil for brushing
16 large boiled sweets
23 cm (9 in) square
  Madeira cake (see p. 24)
  or Quick cake mix (see
  p. 22)
450 ml (15 fl oz) double
  cream
8 tablespoons lemon curd
225 g (8 oz) yellow
  almond paste
Icing sugar for dusting
Selection of spring flowers

With its fresh spring flowers, soft pastel colours and lemony, almond flavour this cake is not only perfect for the Easter holiday celebrations, but for any springtime occasion that warrants a special cake. The most intriguing aspect of the cake is its 'stained glass' decoration. (See the photograph on p. 80.) This is simply made by melting boiled sweets on a sheet of foil. Initially the sweets bubble and boil as they melt into each other and then they set to a beautiful clear glaze that's quite effortlessly lifted to the top of the cake once cooled. Use translucent boiled sweets, preferably from a pick-and-mix counter if you want to be selective about your colour choice.

Choose flowers to tie in with the colours of the sweets (or vice versa if you have a particular flower in mind). Freesia, primula, primrose, apple, almond or orange blossom are all very pretty. So that the flowers are not wasted, leave the stems quite long – then they can be lifted from the cake and returned to a small vase after the party.

*1* Pre-heat the oven to gas mark 6, 400°F (200°C). Line the base of the cake tin with foil and brush the foil lightly with a little oil. Arrange the sweets in rows over the foil, mixing up the colours as much as possible (see drawing). Place in the oven for 10–20 minutes until the sweets have melted and cover the base of the tin. (The cooking time may vary considerably, depending on the type of sweets used.) Leave the sweets to cool completely in the tin.

*2* Using a large knife take a thin slice off the top of the cake to make it completely flat, then slice the cake in half horizontally. Whip the cream with 5 tablespoons of the lemon curd until just holding its shape. Use the remaining lemon curd and a little of the whipped cream to sandwich the cake halves together. Place on a plate or board.

*3* Using a palette knife, spread the remaining cream mixture over the top and sides of the cake to cover completely.

*4* Roll out the almond paste on a surface dusted with icing sugar and cut out a 23 cm (9 in) square. Cut this into 4 equal strips and secure one strip to each side of the cake.

*5* Peel the foil away from the hardened sweets and lay over the cake, pressing down gently. Use the flowers to decorate the top edges of the cake.

**EQUIPMENT**

*23 cm (9 in) square cake tin*
*Sheet of foil*
*Large sharp knife*
*28 cm (11 in) square silver cake board or large flat plate*
*Palette knife*
*Rolling-pin*

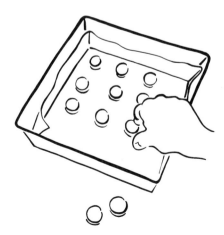

*Arrange the boiled sweets in a cake tin lined with lightly oiled foil.*

# TEMPLATES

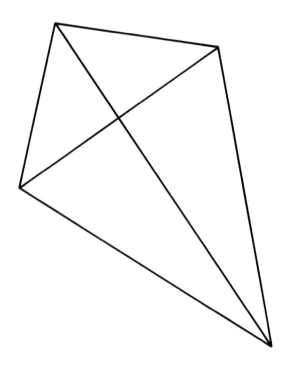

*Kite template for the Flying kite cake on page 58.*

*Butterfly wings template for the Sunflower cake on page 64.*

# LIST OF SUPPLIERS

CRAY CAKE CRAFT
66 High Street
St Mary Cray
Kent
BR5 3NH
Tel: 0689 827234

THE GROVE BAKERY
AND CAKE ARTISTRY
CENTRE
28–30 Southbourne
Grove
Southbourne
Bournemouth
Dorset
BH6 3RA
Tel: 0202 422653

HOMEBAKERS SUPPLIES
157–159 High Street
Wolstanton
Newcastle-Under-Lyme
Staffordshire

B. R. MATTHEWS
AND SON
12 Gypsy Hill
Upper Norwood
London
SE19 1NN
Tel: 081 670 0788

DAVID MELLOR
4 Sloane Square
London
SW1W 8EE
Tel: 071 730 4259

SQUIRES KITCHEN
SUGARCRAFT
Squire House
3 Waverley Lane
Farnham
Surrey
GU9 8BB
Tel: 0252 734309

WOODNUTT'S LTD
97 Church Road
Hove
Sussex
BN3 2BA
Tel: 0273 205353

# INDEX

Page numbers in *italic* refer to colour photographs or illustrations

QUICK & EASY CAKE DECORATING